# READING, WRITING, AND THE EXCEPTIONAL CHILD

## A Psycho-socio-linguistic Approach

**M. Suzanne Hasenstab**

University of Virginia
Charlottesville, Virginia

**Joan Laughton**

Northwestern State University
Natchitoches, Louisiana

AN ASPEN PUBLICATION®
Aspen Systems Corporation
Rockville, Maryland
London
1982

Library of Congress Cataloging in Publication Data

Hasenstab, M. Suzanne
Reading, writing, and the exceptional child.

Bibliography
Includes Index
1. Handicapped children—Education—Language arts.
I. Laughton, Joan. II. Title.
LC4028.H37        371.9′044        82-3974
ISBN: 0-89443-654-6              AACR2

Publisher: John Marozsan
Editorial Director: R. Curtis Whitesel
Managing Editor: Margot Raphael
Editorial Services: Jane Coyle
Printing and Manufacturing: Debbie Swarr

Library of Congress Catalog Card Number: 82-3974
ISBN: 0-89443-654-6

*Printed in the United States of America*

1   2   3   4   5

*To Chris, Michael, Sally, and the world-famous authors*

*C an this book, written in two small university towns in the South, provide happiness as an aid to teachers of reading?*

# Table of Contents

# Acknowledgments

The authors wish to acknowledge Dr. Richard R. Kretschmer for inspiring us to write the book we had been discussing for years. We wish to thank Gary Jones for his input in Appendix B. Special thanks go to our typists, Becky Markwell and Becky Shifflett. Additionally, we thank Lisa Wood and Nancy Jones for their library and copying efforts.

# Chapter 1

# Taking a Position

$O$*nce upon a time . . .*

## INTRODUCTION

Reading, the topic of this book, is certainly not a novel issue. It has been repeatedly addressed in the literature in attempts to define the process, to provide guidance in instruction, and to determine the techniques of assessing reading ability. Throughout history, reading has been the badge of intellect and the proof of knowledge and education. In early societies, the person with a mastery of written language was a respected and valued citizen. Today, the ability to read is a means of survival in our complex daily lives.

There is little doubt that reading is indeed necessary. This, however, may be one of the few facts about which professionals of various disciplines can agree. The present state of the art in reading is plagued by conjecture and disagreement owing to differences in philosophical bases and the limitations imposed by discipline emphases and the resulting points of view.

As one reviews the available literature, both recent and historical, it becomes obvious that there is really nothing definitive regarding the phenomenon we call reading. Definitions, approaches, and proposed panaceas have emerged and waned; and yet professionals continue to be dismayed by the "how tos" of teaching reading and the obvious failures that they face.

## PURPOSES

A major purpose of this book is to provide a framework and to suggest some implications for the teaching of reading to children with exceptionalities. These children require intervention and instruction based on a

3

comprehensive psycho-socio-linguistic foundation. Models and methods that have approached the reading process as a series of unrelated parts rather than as a conceptual whole have been relatively ineffective with such children. Many children who have difficulties in reading are not labeled as exceptional. Both of these populations, labeled and unlabeled, are addressed by this book.

Hopefully, early utilization of our model and procedures can reduce the number of children who experience reading failure. Extending that perspective, all children can be "taught" how to read using the principles described here. Throughout the book, we refer to successful readers and those having reading difficulties rather than to exceptional children. Some illustrations are drawn from various labeled exceptional groups, but our assumption is that reading does not become a different process because a different label is applied to each student.

The focus of the book is derived from a broad psycho-socio-linguistic orientation, and we attempt to define reading from this perspective. We also present an overview of the evolution of trends in reading instruction and methodologies and of their respective benefits and limitations. The main thrust is the presentation of a model developed by the authors to depict the process of reading. An elaboration of the model is applied to reading evaluation and instruction.

## ASSUMPTIONS

Certain tenets underlie the definition, model, and their implications:

- All children possess a facility for reading mastery as part of the linguistic function.
- Reading is a linguistic process, not a set of skills to be achieved.
- Current reading instruction frequently emphasizes inappropriate strategies in learning to read.
- A broad psycho-socio-linguistic approach to reading is an appropriate base for methodology.

## FORMING A DEFINITION OF READING

Definitions of reading abound in the literature; they range from simplistic direct explanations to highly complicated interrelationships of many contributing factors. At an oversimplifed level, reading has been equated with wordnaming or wordcalling. At this level, reading includes only the correct pronunciation of a written form. No comprehension of the word meaning is considered necessary. An extension of this definition would be the correct pronunciation of the word aloud by the reader followed by a recognition (comprehension) of that word as it is known from spoken vocabulary.

Other straightforward explanations include reading as a process of reasoning (Thorndyke, 1917) or the ability to glean meaning from printed symbols by putting meaning into them (Dale, 1976). Reading has also been regarded as speech written down.

Reading at a more complex level has been defined as a set of "skills" (Kirk, 1962) that relate to auditory and visual processing and cognition. Viewing reading from a global point of view, Spache and Spache (1969) consider reading to be a multifactored process. Therefore, in their view a single definition of such a process would be inadequate. They view reading as a process of stages or developmental skills that culminate in reading mastery. The ability to communicate intact perceptual processes, experiential opportunities, cognitive ability, and other aspects all operate in and contribute to the reading definition.

Carroll (1964) defines reading as the "activity of reconstructing (overtly and covertly) a reasonable spoken message from a printed text, and making meaningful responses to the reconstructed message that would be made to the spoken message" (p. 62). This explanation could imply that the reader's ability to comprehend and describe the printed information is highly related to codability of the meaning in language.

Investigations in the area of linguistics and the study of language acquisition have sparked a new trend in reading definition. Kretschmer (1979) defines reading as a process of abstracting meaning from the printed page. F. Smith (1973) and K. Goodman and Niles (1970) present reading as a psycho-socio-linguistic process that emerges from the mutual interaction of language and thought. Their focus is primarily on the derivation of meaning (semantics) from the form (syntax) of written language. Hodges and Rudorf (1972) also support a view of reading as a "language based process" (p. viii). Another linguistic definition is proposed by Gormley and Franzen (1978) in their description of reading as a language process involving active reconstruction of meaning by the reader. These definitions are well summarized by McKenzie (1977) in the statement that "reading is concerned with processing written language, not with identifying words. The learner must make generalizations and infer the rules [of language] that operate" (p. 316).

Difficulties with many earlier definitions stem, first of all, from the tendency to describe one aspect of the reading process that is then applied by practitioners as a new, novel, or somehow magic potion for learning to read or for curing ills of reading failure. Another difficulty emerges from descriptions of reading that are so global that nearly any form of reading instruction could rationally be fitted to the definition.

In the present context, we consider reading to be a form of communication between an author and a reader. From this perspective, the reading process has been incompletely or narrowly viewed by some educators (teachers of reading) as a struggle by the reader to determine meaning from printed text. On the other hand, another set of educators (teachers of writing) have been concerned with the writer's perspective in presenting meaning in written form. Communication implied between these two components can be facilitated by a perspective of communicative interaction between writer and reader. This is really a type of *conversation* between the two parties. In written conversation as in spoken conversation, there are rules to be followed to ensure that the message is delivered and received by both participants. However, there is an important difference. The rules for conversation in spoken and written language are not synonymous; that is, there are different requirements related to the sense of audience or the presuppositions about the audience. In written communication, the audience is unavailable to provide feedback to the author; therefore the author spends more words setting the scene and presenting information to ensure comprehension by the reader. In spoken interactions, such protocol would not be necessary because the speaker and listener could discern major factors in the communication activity; for example, is the listener nodding the head in understanding, scowling in disagreement, or questioning with the eyes in misunderstanding?

Spoken conversations are the result of the simultaneous use of pragmatic, semantic, syntactic, and phonologic knowledge and information about language. Written language employs these systems in addition to an orthographic system. As a spoken conversation takes on the various forms contingent upon the speaker's underlying intent, written conversation can be observed to operate in a similar fashion. Conversations, both spoken and written, have cohesive elements that are dictated by purpose; for example, an argument uses a rather different syntactic form and different lexical items and phonological selection than does a greeting conversation.

For the purposes of this text, reading is simply defined as a conversation between author and reader. The elaborated definition constitutes the contents of this book.

## OVERVIEW OF CHAPTERS

In this first chapter, we have presented some of the definitions that have been offered regarding reading. We have also presented our definition and the underlying assumptions of that definition that form the foundation for the book.

Chapter 2 briefly addresses the major trends in approaches to the teaching of reading and the underlying motivations or philosophies that govern the various approaches. The dichotomy between phonics and whole-word views is examined, as well as the issue of "decoding to the auditory," a strategy that has held the attention of reading professionals for the past 50 years.

The heart, so to speak, of the book is Chapter 3. The purposes of this chapter are (1) to acquaint the reader with aspects of psycho-socio-linguistic theory related to the process of reading and (2) to formulate a model based on this information. The model is of an interactive nature, illustrating the psycho-socio-linguistic components as representative of strategies applicable to the evaluation and instruction of reading.

Chapter 4 expands the model application as related to the determination of preschool children who may be "at risk" for reading difficulty or failure.

Reading evaluation and reading disability are examined in Chapter 5. The most common forms of standardized reading evaluation instruments that have been used traditionally or that are currently in use are presented and discussed. The model is applied with respect to a psycho-socio-linguistic view for the evaluation of reading, and suggestions are presented for alternative methods of assessing reading ability.

Chapter 6 applies the model of the reading process to the issues and concerns of reading instruction. The central focus is the application of the psycho-socio-linguistic levels or strategies to the task of teaching reading. The importance of a "metareading knowledge base" is stressed as vital to the success of young readers.

Written expressive language is dealt with in Chapter 7. Since reading is the receptive form of printed language, its counterpart, writing, should also receive attention. We believe that mutual development of both the input and output forms of written language will facilitate sophistication in both.

The final chapter is a collection of quotations from our experiences with children and adults concerning various aspects of reading. They illustrate lucidly the combined complexity, simplicity, pleasure, and frustration that the learning and teaching of reading represents.

# Chapter 2

# Current Practice in Reading Instruction

*M any years ago, in a faraway land . . .*

## APPROACHES TO TEACHING READING

Professionals charged with the task of teaching reading can readily attest to the availability of the many approaches represented by commercially offered programs. There is no paucity of programs, materials, suggested activities, and so on, that a teacher might select, based on various approaches or theories. Of the many methods and reading approaches that have emerged over time, some have gained and maintained considerable popularity, while others have enjoyed only brief or limited acceptance. Each camp, however, boasts its supporters, suffers its critics, and claims to provide assistance in the instruction and learning of reading. Each approach offers "proof" of positive results when the program is used in the prescribed manner. What may initially appear to be a shopper's paradise in the selection of reading instructional approaches, however, may in reality merely illustrate that the problem of why and how some children learn to read and others do not has yet to be solved to any satisfactory degree.

The approaches and underlying theories in the instruction and mastery of reading have been summarized over the past two decades by many authors in the field (Aukerman, 1971; Chall, 1967; Fries, 1963; Howes & Darrow, 1968; N. Smith, 1963; Strang, 1968; Wolf, 1977). Therefore, we will not present here an exhaustive overview of representative methodology. Rather, general categories of reading theories and their related approaches or methods will be briefly discussed.

### Phonics

One of the most controversial issues related to reading instruction centers on the approaches based on phonics. Questions arise as to how extensive phonics instruction should be, how early it should be employed, and, indeed, whether it is even a feasible approach to teaching reading.

The purpose of phonics is to provide the reader with a set of usable rules that will allow prediction of how a word will be pronounced or "sound," based on how it appears in print or, more specifically, how it is spelled.

Up until the 1920s, phonics was the prevailing method; it is still considered to be an integral aspect of most basal and supplementary reading series. During the 1920s and 1930s, however, as the "reading for meaning" camps, which emphasized a whole-word and vocabulary approach, began to gain popularity, the pure phonics approach became drastically modified and was edged away from the limelight. Then, emphasis was placed on recognition of whole words before letters and sound values were taught. Vocabulary was introduced with meaning at a word level.

In the mid-1950s, the debate between phonics and meaning as a basis for reading instruction was revived. The reaction was aimed primarily at a seeming neglect of a code and letter-sound relationship. A return to phonics was called for, based primarily on work like that of Flesch (1955), who argued that the reason children did not learn to read was due to the "meaning" or whole-word approach. Various alternatives have since been proposed, but phonics still permeates reading instructional practice.

Phonics can appear deceptively easy to the accomplished reader with a sophisticated spoken and written vocabulary, in contrast with the beginning reader who is still restricted in both verbal and printed word exposure. For the veteran reader, phonics can serve as a way to match the printed representation of a word to one that is already familiar and comprehended in an auditory/verbal repertoire. The new reader, who is comparatively inexperienced linguistically, may not have this benefit of prior experience; therefore the word, either spoken or written, may represent a new concept, a new idea. In such cases, phonics does not serve much purpose. This is an especially crucial issue with hearing- and language-disordered children.

The value of phonics in the effective mastery of learning to read has long been a debatable issue. Sexton and Herron (1928) stated that phonics was of little value to beginning readers at Grade 1 but could be beneficial in reading instruction at Grade 2. Also, supporting a delay in the use of phonics in an early reading program, Garrison and Heard (1931) suggested that phonics should not be employed until Grade 3. This view still finds acceptance. Robinson (1971) supports the use of phonics with children who have already learned to read as one alternative in determining the pronunciation of new words. Heilman (1968) agrees that phonics is only one strategy of several that a reader may employ to determine word pronunciation and adds that phonics should not be employed as an approach in the teaching of reading.

Phonics can be helpful in providing a clue to reading in regard to the pronunciation of a visual word configuration in a reading passage. However, if a reader relies heavily on phonics, it may produce such a delay that short-term memory capacity will become so overloaded that the reader will actually lose the meaning or "sense" of what is being read. This is especially true with very young or beginning readers for whom the rate in reading is already quite slow.

In this regard, F. Smith (1973) cites three areas of difficulty related to the use of phonics:

1. the extremely large number of rules that represent verbal pronunciation of printed words
2. knowledge of when these particular rules apply in grapheme/phoneme transfer
3. knowledge of the exceptions to the rules of pronunciation and where and how they apply

In the light of these points, phonics must be seen in reality as being only a probabilistic method of determining word pronunciation from printed representation. The great complexity of the American English sound system makes it extremely difficult to learn and then retain the rules and their inevitable exceptions as required by a phonics emphasis.

### The "Linguistic" Approach

The so-called linguistic approach that emerged during the 1960s varies from phonics in that words that represent consistent common spelling patterns are initially presented. In these spellings, a certain letter always represents a certain sound. However, emphasis is still on code rather than on meaning. Early work by Bloomfield (1942) stressed that focus in reading instruction should be code related. He argued that, because a child has a proficient spoken language based in meaning, the stressing of comprehension in reading instruction is not necessary. The child will eventually grasp meaning from an existing language base. Bloomfield recommended that words with regular spellings be used for initial teaching so that the child could discover sound-letter relationships. In contrast to phonics, "sounding and blending" were omitted, and words were to be read as complete entities. In this approach, new words are spelled, not sounded out.

The linguistic approach, fostering code learning through discovery and internalization of sound-letter association, is based on letter clusters or "families" rather than individual sounds. This view was adopted and formed the basis for several reading systems (Fries, Fries, Wilson & Rudolph, 1966; Lefevre, 1964; Rasmussen & Goldberg, 1965; Richardson, Smith, & Weiss, 1965; Stratemeyer & Smith, 1963). Although this orientation differs from phonics, it is still based on the premise that spoken and written language codes are mutually exchangeable and that written form is dependent upon spoken form. Therefore, the sound-symbol relationship remains paramount.

## Decoding to the Auditory

### Decoding versus Recoding

Our discussion of phonics and the so-called linguistic approach quite logically brings us to the issue of decoding. Currently there is still argument as to whether or not a reader must decode, or rather recode (K. Goodman, 1973), the printed symbol to its auditory counterpart in order for comprehension of a written word to occur. Perhaps, however, before addressing the central issue of the necessity of such action, we should clarify the difference in the meaning of decoding and recoding. We have chosen to adopt the view of K. Goodman (1973) and F. Smith (1973) that decoding implies the transfer from a code to something other than a code, usually meaning. However a transfer from written language (a code) to spoken language (also a code) actually represents a recoding of information, not a decoding. *Decoding, by definition, always terminates in meaning.* The matching of printed forms to spoken forms does not guarantee such results. Based on this orientation, we can examine the need for an exchange from visual to auditory modes to determine meaning.

### Is Recoding to the Auditory Necessary for Meaning?

In addressing this question, a basic premise must be understood. Although speech and the printed word form are both language, written language is not speech written down. Written language is not a reliable representation of sounds resulting in words in speech, nor is the reverse true. We can recode or transfer written language to spoken language, or vice versa, but the transfer must be mediated through meaning. In other words, the decoding of one form, interpreting meaning, must be accomplished before true recoding to another form can occur.

F. Smith (1973) stresses that it is not the change from the written to the spoken form that unlocks meaning, but rather that meaning derived from printed words actually permits the basis for transfer to the sound system.

For example, meaning derived from the semantic-syntactic role of individual words as they relate in a sentence allows for the application of innovative patterns when the sentence is spoken. This also occurs with syllable stress and pronunciation at the individual word level, as in *excuse* as opposed to *excuse*. It is the clarity of meaning, usually derived from sentence context, that clues pronunciation and accent or stress protocol. In addition, the fact that the interrelationships between the written and spoken forms of English and other alphabetic linguistic systems do not represent a simple phoneme-grapheme correspondence means that individual phonemes or letters cannot exist meaningfully out of context or outside the full system of constraints in which they are found.

Based on this orientation, a transfer from visual to auditory symbols is not necessary to determine meaning. In fact, in order to achieve an accurate and understandable recoding from one form to another (visual to auditory or vice versa), meaning must already exist. This view centers on comprehension as central to reading. Word recognition that entails only word pronunciation is not reading. Likewise, children who merely read words in sentences or paragraphs without understanding are not by definition reading or decoding. As illustrated in Figure 2–1, they are merely recoding visual symbols (graphemes) into auditory representation (phonemes).

## COMPREHENSION AND CURRENT READING PRACTICE

The central approach that permeates the teaching of reading at present is based on the design of basal readers. In some ways this approach may be seen as a middle-of-the-road position. Phonics and recoding to the auditory representation of language are considered to be vital skills, but comprehension is also considered to be important. Caution, however, must be exercised in the use of the term *comprehension*, particularly with regard to the underlying interpretation in basal reading programs as to what constitutes comprehension and how it is measured.

As Jenkins, Stein, and Osborn (1981) point out, there is a paucity of research data to evaluate the effectiveness of various commercial reading programs as related to comprehension. They conclude that the existing research has both "design flaws and . . . limited efficacy" (p. 34). An important conclusion is that the existing programs they examined are not designed to teach comprehension. They suggest that more research be undertaken on the effectiveness of commercial reading programs. The questions posed by these authors include:

- "Do programs designed to teach reading and language comprehension live up to their claims?

**Figure 2–1**    Recoding Visual Symbols into Auditory Representation

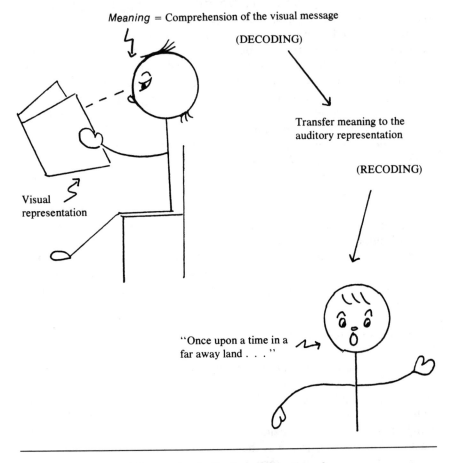

- "Are some programs more effective than others?
- "Are initial effects of programs sustained after the program is removed?
- "Do language oriented programs . . . enhance reading comprehension?" (p. 38)

Because we are also concerned about comprehension as defined by basal readers, we can pose these additional questions:

- How do reading programs view comprehension—as word meaning, matching pictures to words and/or sentences, answering questions, making implications?

- Are the criteria for evaluating a reader's comprehension in reading appropriate? Are they really examining an understanding of written language?
- Do instructional methodologies truly foster strategies for the accomplishment of meaning from written language?

Although meaning or comprehension may be designated as an objective of a reading program, this does not guarantee that the structure and format will allow such goals to be achieved in practice.

## SYSTEMS DESIGNED FOR BEGINNING READERS

The extent of the debate between proponents of phonics and supporters of a meaning approach becomes evident when one investigates the variety of reading systems that have emerged in the past 30 years. Some represent the prominent opposite ends of the continuum, but most fall into line somewhere between the opposing viewpoints.

From a child-centered comprehension base, Ashton-Warner (1963) emphasizes the use of words in beginning reading that are personally significant to a child. Based on this line of reasoning, a system emerged based on the "responsive environment," stressing child initiative (Moore, 1963). The current language experience approach is also founded on an orientation of child-determined direction in reading instruction (Stauffer, 1980).

Examples of systems that are more code oriented include those that foster what Strang (1968) calls the "sound of language" methods. In these approaches, the child listens to another person read aloud and follows the spoken words in the story. The child makes sound-letter associations when possible. A more structured system is the format of Hay and Wingo (1954), in which the child initially associates each consonant sound with each vowel sound. These associations are then presented in the form of a consonant-vowel-consonant (CVC) pattern word.

In some instances, phonics systems have employed visual cues such as drawings or pictures to aid the child in learning the code. The Phonovisual Method (Schoolfield & Timberlake, 1960) teaches each sound separately in a key word represented by a picture. Drill is based on the key words before actual reading instruction occurs. The system of Laubach, Kirk, and Laubach (1967) emphasizes a sequence that begins with the drawing of an item that resembles a letter and with a corresponding target symbol,

such as for a. The next step presents the name of the item,

followed by the upper- and lower-case letter form, the word, and finally the word in sentence context. Spalding and Spalding (1969) advocate a similar system but add the activity of writing letters both in isolation and in word context. Following the linguistic approach, Daniels and Diack (1962) teach sound-symbol associations through regular spellings of words.

A more elaborate use of visual clues, specifically through pictures, is evident in the system by Gibson and Richards (1959). Simple sketch drawings depict information as clues to words and sentences. This format is naturally based on an approach that is more comprehension oriented.

Other early reading approaches, such as the commercially popular Doman (1964) method, emphasize the learning of whole words as entities. Gradually, the child arrives at an understanding of sound-symbol relationships and can determine new words through a process of analysis and synthesis.

## SUMMARY

It is clearly evident that reading has been and is currently taught by many different methods based on various approaches along a continuum with a strong phonics philosophy at one end and a meaning or comprehension base at the other. Despite the overwhelming diversity of theory and practice, none of the resulting approaches has successfully unlocked the secrets of reading mastery. Although we know that children can and do learn to read, we do not understand how this learning comes about. As a result, much of the theory and resulting practice has not reflected success equal to the effort involved.

# Chapter 3

# The Model

*T here lived a handsome prince . . .*

## A MODEL FOR READING

Many theories that attempt to describe the reading process allude to the influence of language competence as the underlying base for reading success. The problem is that these theories then proceed to focus on a single aspect of language such as phonology (through phonics), syntax (via cloze techniques), or semantics (in a word or vocabulary emphasis) rather than attempt to integrate all currently described components of language into a comprehensive reading process model. Many people interested in reading refer to the effect of language on the reading process, but few attempt to delineate the specifics of that relationship. Shuy (1977) states that "one of the more obvious aspects of the act of reading . . . is that, in some mysterious way, the knowledge the reader possesses of his language is called upon and made use of'' (p. vi). He further notes that the attention that has been directed to the linguistic aspects of reading has been "superficial, fragmented, and misguided'' (p. vi) and has been in fact no more than a trivialization of a linguistic approach, consisting primarily of low level phonic issues rather than the more central linguistic issues like meaning and function.

Our model emphasizes simultaneous rather than sequential use of psycho-socio-linguistic subsystems for the process of reading. We take issue with the common assumption that written language, or reading, is spoken language written down. We believe instead that both reading and spoken language tap into a general language awareness. The process of decoding meaning that we present here incorporates a set of hypothesis-testing strategies to be used by readers rather than the traditional skill-oriented viewpoint that emphasizes primarily a grapheme-phoneme exchange.

## FOUNDATIONS

### Historical Viewpoints

The view held by Fries (1963), which, as we have seen, underlies the movement toward a linguistic reading approach, focuses on the absolute identity of the codes of spoken and written language. The reader, according to Fries, responds to "the same set of language signals of the same language" (p. 119). The difference is in the input avenue of sight versus audition. Words are only new representations for a code already in existence in spoken language. Fries, like Bloomfield (1963), also stresses that written language is dependent upon spoken language and is therefore secondary. Bloomfield, however, allows reading even less status, refering to it as "a way of recording language by means of visible marks" (p. 21). This view has dominated views on reading until recently. Today, reading is considered a topic worthy of investigation in its own right, sharing the attention with, but not identical to, spoken language.

We have already stressed that a direct transfer between graphemes and phonemes is not possible. It is our contention, and indeed that of others we have noted, that spoken and written forms or codes of language are parallel but not identical communications with the same meaning or linguistic base. One is not subordinate to or necessarily dependent upon the other. There is indeed a connection between written language and speech, but it is far more complex than originally thought.

### Reading as a Linguistic Process

The relationships between language and reading must be addressed prior to the delineation of objectives or abilities to be acquired and the subsequent design of activities to meet such objectives in reading. Reading has been described as a visual-graphemic representation of language that involves more than a simple one-to-one correspondence between letter configurations and linguistic referents or concepts (Snyder, 1978). Because the reader uses cognitive, linguistic, and experiential knowledge to construct or impose meaning onto printed matter, the process is, obviously, more complex than traditional theory would allow.

Several requisite processes seem to recur in the literature as significant aspects of reading: decoding, word access, syntactic relations, and constructive comprehension processes (Snyder, 1978). Each of these relates in some way to language and the linguistic components.

Decoding, as we have noted, is commonly applied to represent the transfer from the visual code (letters and words in print) to the auditory code (sounds of phonemes and words). To reiterate, this is actually recoding. Decoding requires a termination in meaning that recoding cannot supply.

Word access, also called word retrieval, is also related to reading. Essentially, it concerns the ability to extract meaning from the memory lexicon. It is a matchup of the printed word with a concept or idea.

Attention has also been directed to the syntactic relations of words in sentences and to the constraints and effects these interactions have on meaning. Word meanings are affected by the position they hold in a sentence or phrase and by the other words that co-occur in that context.

The components of language—syntax, semantics, pragmatics and graphophonology—are mutually interdependent; therefore, observation of one necessitates attention to the others (Wardbaugh, 1969). In regard to the activity of reading, Wardbaugh contends that the reader uses "visual clues of spelling, . . . knowledge of probabilities of occurrence, . . . contextual pragmatic knowledge and . . . syntactic and semantic competence to give meaningful interpretation to the text" (p. 133). Reading then is a complex linguistic activity, highly dependent on a child's overall language ability, cognitive functioning, and experience and knowledge of the world. In the mastery of reading, children employ all the components of language as they occur in written language format (Wisher, 1976).

### The Format of Written Language

Since we have taken the position that reading is not spoken language written down, it is important to note the differences. These differences are manifest primarily in the structure or form of the code in which language is expressed, even though spoken language and written language share underlying intents or purposes and the constraints of each of the linguistic components. Reading then cannot feasibly be taught as a visual one-to-one match with the auditory representation of spoken language, since the printed page offers its own mechanisms or structure for coding meaning.

Reading and writing are different from interpersonal communication. The unit for consideration is the conversation or discourse. Spoken conversations may be of many types, depending on underlying intents. They may be argumentative, question-answer, control, persuasive, or ritualistic conversations. The rules used by the participants in the conversation are dependent on the type of conversation. For example, the general format of an argument would include a provoke, a counter, an escalation, slander by both parties, an overture, and a reconciliation (Kretschmer, 1980). A written conversation may be in the form of an essay, a story, or a letter; or it may be an informative item, as in newspapers, signs, and public notices. An example of written language in essay format would include an introduction to the topic, a statement of the problem, a formulation of hypotheses, a review of the literature to justify the hypotheses, data or information presentation, results, conclusions, and implications (Kretschmer, 1980).

Another significant difference between spoken and written conversations is illustrated by the common ways of opening a conversation, negotiating a topic for discussion, changing topics, and closing the conversation. In spoken language, the interaction might be as follows:

$S_1$—Hi, how are you?
$S_2$—Fine, how about yourself?
$S_1$—Not bad, I just got back from Colorado.
$S_2$—Oh!
$S_1$—Yep, went skiing for a week.
$S_2$—I didn't get a vacation this year. I worked.
$S_1$—Well it's nice to be back at work.
$S_2$—Well, I guess I'd better let you go now.
$S_1$—See you around.
$S_2$—Right. Have a good day.

While this is an abbreviation of a potential conversation that really did not ever get a topic negotiated, it served the purpose of brief social interaction. It thus demonstrates the suggestion of a topic, rejection of that topic, an alternative topic, and so on, in spoken conversation.

In written conversation, the author does not negotiate with the reader for a topic. The author selects the topic, and the only negotiation with the reader occurs in terms of keeping the reader's attention or negotiating to select or read another book. The topic in written language is frequently described in much greater detail by the author. It reflects the author's presuppositions about the reader in terms of whether the latter is a 6-year-old, first-grade student or a graduate student in the hard sciences. However, because it is not possible to get feedback from the reader as to the latter's comprehension of the intended message, the author attempts to make certain the message is conveyed by describing it in greater detail.

### Hypothesis Testing

Reading is a hypothesis-testing process. The child is active in the process, that is, the child imposes meaningful organization on incoming stimuli. The task of the teacher or evaluator is to determine what strategies and knowledge the child brings to the learning situation. Kretschmer (1979) describes learning as a process of establishing organizational structures to enhance the ability to predict experiences. This process, when applied to reading, begins with the formulation of hypotheses to reduce uncertainty. Obviously, the quality of these hypotheses is dependent on the quality and quantity of previous experience as well as the organizational capabilities of the learner. This includes the facility with which the learner responds to feedback or error by modifying the hypotheses. Hypothesis generation and testing appear to be present at birth or soon thereafter (Bruner, Goodman, & Austin, 1966; Parrill-Burnstein, 1981); even low-functioning children engage in hypothesis testing.

Two kinds of hypotheses can be seen to contribute to reading: first, those common to all children, irrespective of the experience provided (developmental milestones); and second, those unique to individuals (idiosyncratic) (Kretschmer, 1979). Children with reading disabilities probably develop maladaptive hypotheses that do not serve them well in decoding meaning from print. In assessing reading difficulties, it is important to determine whether those difficulties are developmental or idiosyncratic (Kretschmer, 1979).

## MODEL COMPONENTS

Reading taps into a core of linguistic awareness. A synthesis of current theories of reading and related topics suggests a model of reading that includes the following components: text cohesion, pragmatics, semantics, syntax, and graphomorphophonemics (GMP) (Kretschmer, 1979).

### Text Cohesion

Text is defined by Olson (1977) as written prose. However, for our purposes, a more elaborate definition, that presented by Halliday and Hasan (1976), has been adopted. These authors describe text as a three-part entity: a semantic unit, a unit of language in use (not a grammatical unit), and a passage that together form a unified whole. This entity occurs in both spoken and written language.

Text cohesion refers to a tie that relates one sentence to other sentences throughout the paragraph. This may entail a tie to the sentence immediately following, a cataphoric reference; or it may involve a tie to the preceding sentence, an anaphoric reference. It is not always necessary that the direct tie be between sentences tangent to one another. The referential tie may be more remote, occurring between sentences separated by other sentences in the paragraph that add elaborated information. Cohesion is expressed through grammar (grammatical) and vocabulary (lexical).

Text cohesion consists of the physical format of the print and the structure of the information. It may include text framing (e.g., the format of a letter, or the title page of a story book), text outline (rules followed within the conversation), and text strategies (used in the conversation). The reader begins to generate hypotheses about each of these aspects immediately upon approaching the text. These hypotheses assist the reader in developing further hypotheses that are used in determining the meaning of the text. Text cohesion clues the reader to the more specific pragmatic contributions of the text.

## Pragmatics

The pragmatic contributions to the reading process relate to the functions, purpose, style, and register of the written text. These involve initially a conceptualization of what reading is: that is, there is something called reading, people read, and reading involves getting meaning from a page of printed text. Many children become aware of this because parents and others have read to them and because they have observed others reading.

This suggests that many children enter school with considerable knowledge about reading. Parents of children with various types of learning problems have been accused of not reading or of reading less to their children than do parents of children without suspected or confirmed learning problems. It has been suggested that children who already know how to read upon entering school do so as a result of having had an individual tutor (parent, caretaker, or other reader) who has read interesting stories to them in an enjoyable setting with few, if any, demands for performance. Individual tutoring of this type as an instructional strategy is rare in most first-grade reading programs. A series of studies affectionately referred to as the "Rocking Chair Studies" are underway with surrogate parents who read to young hearing-impaired children (in rocking chairs, of course) in a preschool setting to determine the effects of such an introduction to reading on later reading abilities (Laughton, Jones, & McCubbin, in preparation).

### Underlying Intents

One pragmatic aspect of the reading process or conversation involves the underlying intents that are reflected in all aspects from the choice of format (story, letter, play, exposition, etc.) to the selection of syntactic structure. Underlying intents of spoken language have been termed *the illocutionary force of the sentence* (Searle, 1969, 1975). Basically, this represents an implied performative that is embedded in the sentence and may be implicit. An example is the sentence *When will we be finished?* in which the implied performative is the sentence *I ask you something*. Such underlying intents or speech acts, as they are referred to in spoken language, include the declarative (telling), interrogative (asking), request or imperative, expression (of thought or feeling), and promise or permission (Clark & Clark, 1977). These speech acts are conveyed through the surface structure of language, or they may be overridden by contextual clues, such as facial expression or intonation used in spoken language.

## Old and New Information

Sentences may be used to introduce new information and also to refer to that information as old information once the topic has been established. Sentences usually contain a speech act and an action intended for the listener (Kretschmer & Kretschmer, 1978).

## Presupposition

Presupposition is an important aspect of communication. This refers to the assumptions about the listener that are held by the speaker. In both written and spoken language, the author writes or speaks for a specific intended audience. The author's presuppositions about that reader—such as age, interests, knowledge of the world, political viewpoint, and cultural background—influence the choice of everything from the topic to the lexical selections.

## Turntaking

Turntaking in written language differs from that in spoken language. In spoken language, one person speaks, leaves a temporal space for the other to respond, and so on, with the roles of speaker and listener alternating. In written language, the author takes the first turn and keeps it until the end of the writing. Then the reader responds to the author, but not necessarily directly, unless it is through correspondence. The reader may agree or disagree, tell friends about the book, or even terminate the reading. The reader might also write a letter to the author or editor, alter opinions or behavior as a result of reading the book, or generate an antithesis to what has been read.

## Discourse Requirements

Pragmatic considerations in reading also involve discourse requirements in the coding of conversation into linguistic structures. This concerns intersentence relationships that involve the specific mechanisms used to make one sentence in a text relate to another. Discourse requirements are necessary in order to fulfill the purposes of the conversation (Kretschmer, 1979).

## Summary

Children who know how to read (or write) already know pragmatic and text cohesion rules. In other words, they are able to formulate hypotheses that gives them a basic context needed to discern meaning. Children who do not know these rules are too often the very children who do not receive the benefits of appropriate instructional intervention. To date, the primary emphasis in teaching has been on the application of rules that govern the sound-symbol relationships of phonemes and letters. In some cases, rules of syntax have been stressed, but little attention has been given to using pragmatic and text cohesion rules in current reading programs.

## Semantics

The semantic or meaning aspect of the written conversation has been studied primarily from the single-word or vocabulary standpoint. Some attention has also been given to semantic relationships or underlying propositions. Lexical flexibility or a well-developed vocabulary is usually considered to be a mark of good writing and is the greatest contributor to most operationalized definitions of intelligence. Meaning in a broader sense, as in paragraph or complete-text meaning, is the crux of reading, and also the nemesis of many teachers of reading.

## Semantic Propositions

Semantic units in reading include the propositions that are verbal (focusing on the verb of the sentence) or organizing units with their associated nouns. These propositions define or establish the relationship of entities in sentences (Kretschmer, 1979). Sentences may contain numerous propositions, with memory the only constraint on the number allowed. These propositions aid in the comprehension and memory of sentences and text. Sentence comprehension is highly dependent on the context and previous knowledge of the world possessed by the reader (Anderson & Ortony, 1975; Barclay, 1973; Carpenter & Just, 1975).

## Schema Theory

Considerable interest has developed recently in the study of comprehension through analysis of story grammar. This involves uncovering the structures that regulate the organization and retrieval of incoming story information. Schema theory is a major influence on current thought and practice in reading. It has its base in the research on memory, comprehension, and intelligence (Bartlett, 1932; Kintsch & Greene, 1978; Piaget, 1952). Pearson and Spiro (1980) present a model for considering reading comprehension based on schema theory. Schemata are constructs that are applicable to general cognitive activity or information processing. They are similar to concepts but can apply to a wider variety of phenomena. Schemata are derived from experience. Rumelhart (1975, 1977) has described a schema as similar to a play with a plot, a cast of characters and actors. Many stories include the following schema: a hero who appears early and frequently to help define the role of other characters; a series of events that occur and are causally and temporally related; and episodes that occur in unfolding exposition, complication, and resolution.

To illustrate a schema, Pearson and Spiro (1980) present the following example based on a play analogy for the term *buy*: "Any time there is a *buy* schema there must be a buyer, a seller, an object to be purchased, a medium of exchange, and a place of purchase. These entities are comparable to the cast of characters in a play" (p. 73).

Within a particular schema, sequences of events of importance will occur. Pearson and Spiro liken these events or actions to scenes that take place in a play. Schemata, then, can apply to a wide array of actions, occurrences, and events or sequential relationships; they emerge through the depth and quality that an individual experiences in relation to those actions, objects, or events.

Text comprehension has its base in schema theory (Pearson & Spiro, 1980). Kintsch and Greene (1978) describe the role of schemata in the comprehension and recall of stories. Reconstruction of stories that are read or heard are predictable on the basis of a schema. Kintsch and Greene (1978) and Koblinsky, Cruse, and Sugawara (1978) found that readers compose better summaries of stories when they already have the schema or when the schema is predictable. This appears to be a macrovariable in the reconstruction of stories. A schema-based retrieval plan aids reconstruction and has implications for evaluation and instruction (Gromley & Franzen, 1978; Meyer, 1975).

## Story Grammar

Story grammar structure differs somewhat from what has been termed *critical reading skills* by publishers of reading instructional materials. Critical reading skills often include such targets as identifying the main idea; comparing; sequencing; identifying word meaning; evaluating fact and opinion; judging logic, probability, and relevance; drawing conclusions; and summarizing. These skills are assumed to be components of reading comprehension. While they are no doubt significant in comprehension, the current literature on organization and structure would suggest that story grammar (setting the scene, introducing the hero, etc.) not only assists in comprehension but also aids in recall during reconstruction of the story. Hypotheses at the semantic level that a reader could generate might include abstract meanings of words, semantic relationships, propositions, or underlying structures, such as a story schema that involves basic story units and relationships (Mandler & Johnson, 1977).

## Summary

The semantic aspects of the reading process involve more than simple word meanings. They constitute in fact the major aspect of reading: comprehension. We do not consider simple wordcalling or word recognition as reading. Schema theory and current theories and investigations about story grammar seem to hold more potential for understanding the reading process than simple vocabulary acquisition that has been emphasized in the past.

## Syntax

The contributions of syntax, or the base structure with accompanying transformations, to the decoding of meaning have been well described by Smith and Goodman (1971) and F. Smith (1973). Basically, knowledge of spoken syntax provides options to consider in the hypothesis-testing activity of deciphering an unknown word or set of words during reading. In a sentence such as *The boys ran down the* _____,'' most good readers would generate the word *street* or a similar noun on the basis of the provided syntactic information. Syntax, by itself, is probably rather inefficient in decoding meaning, but it can be used as a monitoring or confirming device for interpretations of meaning. It is important to remember that shorter sentences and less complex syntax may be more difficult to understand because less context may be available.

Syntax can be used to cue the reader to the hierarchy of important aspects. In the sentence *The man who bought our house is Harry's boss, the man . . . is Harry's boss* is the main clause and is more important than the secondary or relative clause. In other words, the information contained in the main clause is of a higher priority and is better remembered than the information contained in the subordinate clause (Kintsch, 1974). Syntax allows for a check on the importance of priorities of given information.

An example of a syntactic hypothesis is that any given sentence under consideration follows the typical subject-verb-object order. With a passive sentence, this hypothesis would have to be rejected. Knowledge of syntax allows prediction of various word-order or grammatical relations of sentences.

### Graphomorphophonemics

The graphomorphophonemic (GMP) (Kretschmer, 1979) cues are rules that govern how words are written. They are the written equivalent of spoken phonology, which includes the sense of letters, spelling patterns, punctuation, and pronunciation. GMP can aid in the decoding of written language. The other component strategies that have been presented, however, are more efficient and powerful.

The basic unit of GMP (reception and production) is the syllable. Unfortunately, many teachers of reading have focused on individual phonemes (as beginning consonants, vowels, etc.) rather than on the syllable. The basis for recoding to the auditory system is syllabic, so it seems sensible to use this type of strategy (sounding out new words syllabically rather than phoneme by phoneme). This strategy has been found to have a higher relationship with reading ability (Kretschmer, 1979).

There is some suggestion that, in using a GMP approach, there is not enough context to decode words, since young children initially look for meaning when approaching a text. This would further suggest that children need to know what constitutes a word before they can analyze the components (syllables) and then synthesize these components into a whole word. There is also evidence that suggests that the better readers are those who can best use a GMP strategy (Jenkins et al., 1981). It thus appears that not only is GMP a difficult strategy but that it fails to provide enough context or meaning to be used by less able readers.

### STRUCTURE OF THE MODEL

The components of language as they operate in reading, and therefore in the model, may be seen as analogous to a ladder. Each step or linguistic component presents an access or strategy for reaching the top. The top of the ladder, the ultimate goal in reading, is comprehension, represented by experience, world knowledge, cognition, and so on. One may view comprehension from the GMP step of the reading structure, but there is difficulty in attaining or grasping the full reward at the top of the ladder. Each step or strategy becomes an increasingly more effective entry to reach or decode meaning and attain comprehension. However, the most effective way to master the task is to use the component strategies together, integrating the information or view of comprehension that each affords. This analogy is explained in detail in Chapter 5, where the model is applied in relation to reading instruction. See Figure 3–1 for a depiction of the model's structure.

**Figure 3–1**   The Model

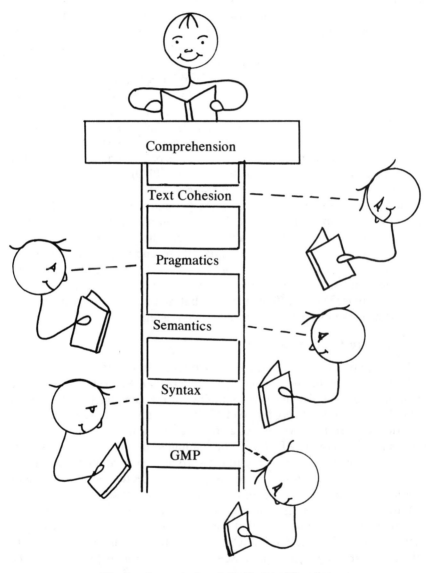

**The Psycho-socio-linguistic Model of Reading**

**Figure 3-1**    continued

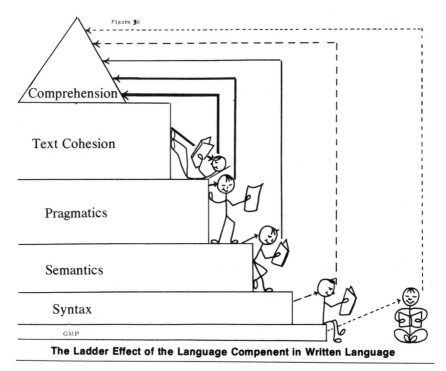

The Ladder Effect of the Language Compenent in Written Language

## Integrated Use of Linguistic Strategies

Successful reading requires the use of all five systems of the model simultaneously, not sequentially, to decode meaning. It is possible that entry into the reading processing system may occur at any point and may be unique for each individual. Based on a multitude of experiential factors, a child may approach the reading of a text using pragmatic, semantic, syntactic, or GMP strategies, depending on preference based on previous instruction. The question is, What is the most efficient entry into the process and what strategies can best facilitate the process? Unfortunately, the most frequently taught strategy, as we have seen, appears to be the phonemic-to-semantic (sound it out to decode meaning) strategy.

## Good Readers

Good readers form hypotheses about all linguistic systems simultaneously. If misunderstanding occurs at any one level, it is appropriate to go to the next system to check the hypothesis. For example, fairy tales have a specific format (text cohesion) that includes an introduction that sets the scene and time briefly and succinctly, as in "Once upon a time, in a far away land. . . . " The fairy tale then usually presents the main character(s) ("There lived a lovely young maiden."), followed by a statement of a problem that dictates the central goal of the story. For example, the statement, " . . . who was kept prisoner by an evil old troll in a very high tower," tells the reader of the maiden's dilemma and infers that the goal is release of the maiden from the troll's evil prison. A series of episodes then follows: "The maiden pleaded with the troll. She offered the evil master all of her earthly belongings. She promised to sing him love ballads every day. . . . " At some point, depending on the complexity and length of the tale, a resolution occurs: "One day a knight in shining armor with a trusty sword slew the evil old troll." Once resolution occurs, a happy ending is ensured, as when "the courageous knight and the beautiful maiden rode off on his magnificent white horse and lived happily ever after."

A good reader might address the activity of recoding such a tale by first examining the title page. One rule of text cohesion (format) is that the title page always comes first. In most cases nonverbal and nonlinguistic clues will accompany the title. Our reader will note, for example, the picture of a castle on a mountain top. This provides clues to very different information about the content than does a picture of a farmyard and a red barn. From this very early information or format, our reader can hypothesize that a fairy tale is to follow. The observations to this point provide the basic context for further hypotheses.

If he has read fairy tales in the past, the reader will bring to the first page an awareness of the underlying intent of such a format. He therefore would immediately sense a violation of that form if the first sentence read, "Many castles were built by the nobility in the 1200s." If he fails to hypothesize correctly at this pragmatic level, he will then begin to search the other linguistic subsystems or strategies to formulate new hypotheses or to confirm his original ideas. When the reader first perused the title page, he determined via text cohesion that the book he had selected was a fairy tale. However, when he read the first sentence, his knowledge of pragmatics and fairy tales failed to bear out his hypothesis.

A more extreme example of a violation of our reader's original hypothesis might be if the first sentence read, "Farmer Jones milks his cows twice each day." Such a sentence would undoubtedly cause our good reader considerable frustration because the information blatantly causes a rejection of his hypothesis. When a reader is able to have his hypothesis supported readily across all linguistic systems, he in turn enjoys reading and may even adopt certain preferences for particular formats or kinds of reading. Reading success is having your hypotheses borne out across all psycho-socio-linguistic levels.

At a semantic level, the good reader would also sense a deviation from his expected fairy tale in the words "nobility . . . castle," in contrast to the more appropriate "troll's castle." He would also be sensitive to the use of "nobility" in lieu of "rich or royal people."

At a syntactic level, the reader would find his hypothesis frustrated by the appearance of an essay structure rather than a structure more characteristic of fairy tales.

> *(adverb—time)*    *(adverb—place)*    *(verb)*
> "Once upon a time, in a far away land, lived a
> *(+ description)*
> lovely young maiden."
>
> *Transformation = adverbial inversion*

In this sentence, the base structure has been transformed by inverting the usual noun phrase + verb phrase + adverbials (NP + VP + adv) to create the fairy tale format.

Now consider the following:

"Many castles were built by the nobility during the 1200s."

In this case, a standard passive transformation is more illustrative of an essay format that might occur in a history text.

If perchance our reader failed to recognize one of the vital introductory words (nobility), he could employ GMP strategies via syllabication, not by a progression of sounding out each individual phoneme, to determine the word.

## Unsuccessful Readers

Now let us consider the not-so-successful reader. This reader, as he selects the same text as the previous reader, usually brings less experiential knowledge as to what reading is about, specifically as applied to fairy tales versus historical essays. As he peruses the title page and notes the castle, this reader may fail to decipher the context portrayed by the castle and therefore will not generate a hypothesis concerning what the text is about. He then approaches the print on the first page without any information available as a result of text cohesion or pragmatic rules and hypotheses.

As he begins to read, he has no context in which to attempt to decode meaning.

If he is able to recognize the introductory words and the beginning sentence, he may be able to use semantic-syntactic hypotheses to begin a rudimentary context so that he can decode meaning. If, however, several words exist in the early text that are unfamiliar to him, he is reduced to dependence on the GMP-level strategies. The chances of this reader achieving comprehension are very slight.

In summary, text cohesion or the physical format helps predict what kind of form is to be read. For example, the following leaves little doubt in most successful readers as to the type of reading required:

7777 Xxxxx Xxxxx
Xxxxx, Xxxx Xxxxx
Xxxxx 77, 7777

Xxxx Xx. Xxxxx:

Pragmatics or the underlying functions needed for information help predict where to go for certain types of reading, for example, where to look if you want to know how to bake an apple pie, which would probably not be in a dictionary.

The reader, as we have noted, can enter the reading activity at any of the linguistic component-levels. For example, a rather sophisticated reader may opt for a syntactic strategy to decode meaning. He reads the first three words, does not recognize the fourth word, and hypothesizes that the unknown word must be a verb because of the structure of what he has already read. A reader entering at a phonemic level recognizes the first word, but not the one immediately following. He then begins to sound out the second word (e.g., m—a—n). He hears himself say the word, comprehends the word, and goes on with his reading. Either of these strategies is appropriate and can be used. However, the issue is: Which of the strategies is most efficient in the reading process?

Unfortunately, a considerable amount of reading instructional time to date has focused on only one or two of the components at a time, that is, phonic or syntactic or semantic in the form of vocabulary development. The apparent assumption has been that the process is sequential and that the elements comprising the sequence are well-delineated. As F. Smith (1973, 1975) has pointed out, if this were an accurate description of the reading process, fewer children should have reading disabilities. However, the converse seems to be true. There seem to be preliminary data to support the position that the reading process might better be viewed as several important systems operating simultaneously rather than sequentially (Kretschmer, 1979).

## Bottom-Up and Top-Down Processing

We have stated that reading is an information processing activity. Information presented on a page and represented by written symbols is visually and linguistically analyzed to determine meaning. It is then utilized in some fashion by the individual, which results in behavior or storage in long-term memory (Hasenstab & Schoeny, 1982). Pearson and Spiro (1980) present two forms of information processing. The first, which is data bound (e.g., the printed information on the page), is termed *bottom-up* or *outside-in* (F. Smith, 1975) processing. This type is considered to be text based in nature. The second type is *top-down* or *inside-out* (F. Smith, 1975) processing. Unlike text-based processing, top-down processing requires that the reader make hypotheses regarding the information based on knowledge already possessed. This knowledge of course results from previous learning and experiences as well as from the values and attitudes the reader has acquired.

To view these processing modes in terms of our model, a bottom-up approach entails the entry and use of the linguistic component strategies to secure meaning and comprehension. Top-down processing places the reader at the top of the ladder as a function of an ability to form various hypotheses concerning text-based information from his knowledge foundation. This reader has an advantage of context. The more context available, the easier the reading activity.

## Context

Context is highly significant in the reading process. It also aids memory. Memory in turn is the storage place for previous learning. The result is almost a circular effect in that each component (context, memory, comprehension) feeds and expands the others.

Context may be provided to the reader either in the print itself or in elaborations by pictures, figures, graphs, tables, and so on. The use of imagery, especially with beginning readers, has been found to enhance both comprehension and story recall (Anderson & Hidde, 1971; Guttman, Levin, & Pressley, 1977; Pressley, 1976). Although context is alluded to in most existing reading methodologies, it is seldom utilized to its full capacity, and therefore full value is not realized.

## SUMMARY

The primary advantage of the model presented in this chapter is that it addresses reading from a comprehensive perspective. All of the recognized components of language are addressed. This is necessary if a complete view of reading as a psycho-socio-linguistic process is to be adopted.

# Chapter 4

# Identification of Children "At Risk" for Reading Problems

*A* dorned in glittering armor . . .

In Chapter 2 we noted the interest that has been generated regarding the importance of the preschool years to later reading achievement. Cognitively oriented preschools claim to encourage approaches that are designed to enhance later reading performance. However, these early programs, referred to as "readiness" programs, typically stress visual and auditory skill development that is either nonlinguistic (as in recognition of environmental sounds) or at a very low phonological level (as in recognition of initial sounds in words or sound/symbol relationships). Early programs that claim to stress language development in early reading focus primarily on vocabulary development. There is very little attention devoted to reading as a comprehensive linguistic process with delineation of all the major subsystems of language (phonology, syntax, semantics, and pragmatics).

In addition to attempts to provide a basis for early reading instruction, many programs also claim to identify children who are potentially at risk for later reading difficulties. Evaluation procedures are often founded on standardized instruments designed to project potential problems or task analysis based on an assumed visual and auditory skill development model with additional attention to vocabulary.

As discussed in Chapter 3, the underlying premise on which the skill model is based is questionable from the point of view of reading as a linguistic process. Therefore, the evaluation and observational procedures emerging from this model must also come under scrutiny. Although evaluation procedures based on the skill model may evaluate some designated auditory and visual skills or survey vocabulary, there is no guarantee that they do, in fact, examine or assess those linguistic aspects that we believe are prerequisites to reading. The purpose of this chapter is to delineate areas arising from the model that can be used to provide prognostic information concerning potential reading success or difficulty.

## THE CHILD AT RISK FOR READING DIFFICULTIES

In developing a systematic approach for determining which children may demonstrate problems in learning to read, we are faced, first of all, with the concept or definition of a child who is "at risk" for reading difficulties. Several hypotheses that attempt to offer a foundation for defining such children may be found in the literature. For example, a child with a mental age of less than 6 years and 6 months might be classified as at risk based on a limitation in cognitive or intellectual functioning (Kirk, Kliebhan, & Lerner, 1978). Other factors that have been suggested as indicative that a child is at risk or a potential reading remediation candidate are cultural deprivation and its effects on intellectual performance, deficiencies in visual-motor areas or skills, various exceptionalities, and social and emotional development (Heber, Barber, Harrington, Hoffman & Fallander, 1972; Kirk, 1965; Kirk & Kirk, 1956; Spache & Spache, 1973; Strang, 1968). We are not saying that such factors cannot or do not affect the child's overall development, knowledge base, and experience; however, these aspects address the issue of reading potential from a rather broad-based reference or a more peripheral point of view. We contend that a more effective manner of defining a child who is at risk with respect to reading difficulties involves looking at specific language-based areas rather than those that may be peripherally or more generally related. Underlying this approach is the view of reading as a mode of language, specifically written language. The specific language-based areas will be discussed as a reinterpretation of the "readiness" concept.

## READINESS—A PERSPECTIVE

The concept, *readiness,* is not new in the literature or in the vocabulary of teachers of preschool or primary-level children. The idea of readiness relates to "a state of development that is needed before a skill can be learned" (Kirk et al., 1978, p. 32). However, it must be emphasized that this state of development does not imply that the mastery of particular skills isolated from one another will guarantee subsequent emergence or development of the behavior, ability, or developmental system. Readiness is seen to be a time in which various skills are consolidated or interrelated so as to allow for the appearance or development of a new or elaborated skill. To expand beyond the skill orientation, readiness can also be considered to be the time in which a child is mastering prerequisite knowledge and experiences that will permit the emergence of new or further developmental behaviors. Readiness is not static; it is a dynamic process. In readiness, the child is actively involved in experiencing, processing, comprehending, modifying, and internalizing information that will allow the child to proceed to the next facet of mastery, development, or maturity. In other words, readiness is a summation of previous and current experience and knowledge to the time at which the child is able to accomplish a new task or master a more sophisticated process.

Readiness is not confined to the prereading period, although reading is the context to which it is most often associated. For example, an individual may be in the state of readiness for reading a novel but not yet in the state of readiness for the mastery of Shakespeare. Readiness in a broad perspective actually applies to any area of development. There is a time of readiness before a child utters a first word, takes a first step or rides the first bicycle. Readiness implies that an event or developmental milestone is a culmination of maturation, experience, and knowledge that a child applies to the mastery of a particular process or ability.

The accomplishment of the first word or first step or any other of a number of firsts mapped along the child's development to adulthood is far from an overnight occurrence; it is based ultimately in what has occurred with the child previously in all areas of growth. For example, the emergence of first words represents approximately a year of "study" by the young child. First utterances result from the interactive maturing of the physiological aspects of the child's growth, including the development of the senses, motor facility and neurological system. These utterances are based on the cognitive experiences and respective learning that occurs, including expanded concepts and schemata as well as the social and linguistic contexts to which the child has been exposed, as these factors apply to the development of the language system. By the time the first true verbal representation of an object, action, or event occurs, the child has hypothesized, experimented, repatterned, verified, and applied all of those aspects necessary to produce first words in an elaborate system of rehearsals. Thus, readiness cannot be viewed as a narrow set of skills that preclude a more elaborate skill. Readiness is a time in which a child develops the realization of what a particular process or function is about. It is a time of awareness.

## Reading Readiness

The period of readiness as applied to reading is seen to be the time in which a child prepares physically, cognitively, socially, and especially linguistically to master the feat of learning to read. Readiness proponents have emphasized that there are prerequisites for the mastery of reading that relate to areas of neurological functioning, auditory and visual efficiency and perception, language and speech development, and social and personal maturity. Strang (1968) presents in her brief overview of reading readiness the following areas that indicate a child's preparedness for reading facility:

- an understanding of spoken words based on firsthand experience
- ability to use a variety of English sentences to communicate ideas
- ability to identify, distinguish, and remember sounds in words
- ability to identify, distinguish, and copy geometric and other shapes
- ability to form concepts by classifying objects in the environment
- ability to use sentence structures that show relationships between ideas
- eagerness for new experiences; curiosity about new things in the environment
- desire to learn to read

Kirk et al. (1978) cite the following areas, suggested by observation and research, as contributing to reading readiness:

- mental maturity
- visual abilities
- auditory abilities
- speech and language development
- thinking skills
- physical fitness and motor development
- social and emotional development
- interest and motivation (p. 33)

Although these factors may bear some relationship to reading readiness from a broad perspective as mentioned earlier, many of them deal with rather peripheral concerns, such as eye-hand coordination, auditory association, visual discrimination, sound blending, auditory closure, and visual association. We prefer to select more specific aspects of language development as the central issue for concern with respect to reading. We would therefore redefine readiness, a period of learning about reading, as the linguistic process that it is. This process would appear to be more appropriately termed *metareading*.

## Metareading

Metareading as an extension of the readiness concept refers to the growing knowledge that the young child possesses about reading as a process. Metareading addresses what the child knows about reading. In other words, metareading involves the process by which children can place themselves in the position of observers of the function; that is, they can step outside the process and observe or analyze the process in action. Examples of the type of learning that a child internalizes during the time of metareading relate to the understanding of the purpose, function, and use of books and other reading materials. Metareading also includes the child's growing concept of pictures and printed words and how they represent meaning. Metareading is a function of repeated exposure to text through handling of books, observing others read, being read to, and pretending to read for oneself. Thus, metareading knowledge comes about as a result of varied and meaningful experiences with reading.

The concept of metareading differs from readiness in its focus on the total linguistic nature of the reading process and in its deemphasis of isolated subskills that have not been conclusively shown to be related to reading. In other words, evaluation and observation of a child's metareading knowledge is directly related to the child's growing repertoire of information about reading and written launguage per se. If reading is considered to be a linguistic process, which is the basic tenet of this book, then it is imperative that evaluation procedures be linguistic as well. Evaluation procedures based on a metareading perspective meet the requirements for identifying potential reading problems more realistically than the broad, peripheral orientation of the current focus and implication of readiness.

It should be noted that although readiness concepts do not totally ignore the aspect of language as important to the mastery of reading, most viewpoints include that aspect primarily as one of a number of components or requirement areas of development that contribute to reading success. Our position focuses on language acquisition as central to the state of metareading and subsequent success in the mastery of acutal reading performance.

**Metareading as an Indicator of High-Risk Children**

Examination of a child's knowledge of the reading process can serve as a helpful indicator of a readiness to read. Linguistically intact children enjoy taking on a metalinguistic role in which they attempt to discover how language functions, what language does, and how they can manipulate their environments with language. This usually takes the form of vocal or verbal play in which children actually play and are then amused by manipulating their own productions. A child as young as 18 months can be heard rehearsing a repertoire of sounds in the context of song or varied intonation patterns, while a slightly more sophisticated 3-year-old plays with words such as *fiddle-faddle* or *middle-maddle*. The preoccupation of primary-level children with rhyming words is also a form of verbal play. With older children, the focal point of jest or humor might actually be dependent upon the subtle selection of an initial sound or point of stress in a word or phrase. This metalinguistic experimentation and discovery also serves as a metareading function.

One signal of a potential at-risk status can be observed in a paucity or restricted use of strategies in connection first with spoken language, then with language in print. Young children develop quite early interest in and strategies for dealing with print. This may be seen as young children point out printed words and attach a label to that print or as they follow the line of print with their finger as they "read" along. Lack of interest in print or restricted use of emerging strategies for imposing meaning on print can point to a possible prereading deficit. The child probably uses a paired-associate strategy in these early readings but later induces the underlying orthographic rules (Stark, 1981). These are rules that allow for reading words that the child has never previously seen in print.

**Metareading Evaluation Tasks**

The preschool teacher or interventionist can stage or design various tasks to observe and evaluate a child's metareading knowledge based on the linguistic subsystems or components of reading. The teacher can also observe as the child interacts or plays with books or other reading materials without guidance or interference from adults. Metareading knowledge can be further observed in a storytelling or storyreading setting where an adult tells or reads a story, book, or other reading passage to a young child. Careful noting of what the child does in these situations and subsequent analysis of the data as related to linguistic aspects of the reading model presented in Chapter 3 will provide a helpful indication of what the child presently possesses regarding knowledge of reading as written language.

*Text Cohesion*

In examining a metareading level of knowledge of text cohesion, the teacher can set up a task in which the child is requested to select or indicate such text-related vocabulary as book, page, words, sentence, title, story, beginning, end, pictures, characters, covers, top, bottom, front, back, and the like. It should be remembered that a preschool child may be unable to verbalize and answer to a question such as, "What is a book?" but can very well indicate knowledge of what a book is by responding appropriately to the directive, "Show me the book." In this task, it is best to use a real book rather than pictures depicting the various text-related concepts. In this way, the child is applying knowledge directly to the book or the focus of the metareading aspect. Directives such as "Show me how to use a book" or "Let's pretend with these books," can elicit behaviors that will demonstrate more precisely what the child knows about reading activity. The quality and sophistication of the child's performance will also suggest the extent of exposure the child has experienced in reading.

In a less structured situation, children could be given books and left to peruse on their own while the teacher observes their interaction with the books. Observation notes should include data as to whether the children correctly position the books, observe and/or point to the pictures, or pretend to read through vocalization or verbalization. If the children are familiar with the books, they may attempt to retell or restructure the story. The manner in which they handle or address the books will reflect their knowledge and experience about the purpose and function of the books as reading material.

An additional context in which to observe a child's awareness of text cohesion at a metareading level is through the interactive setting of an adult reading a story to the child. The child's attentiveness would indicate an understanding of the context in which the child is placed; that is, it is reading time during which quiet, attending behavior is expected. Once again the child's treatment of the book would alert the observer to the child's awareness of the purpose of the material. The child's commentary and nonverbal behavior, such as pointing to or patting pictures in the book, would also be important data. Children may also be encouraged to turn pages, fill in missing words, and indicate the end of the story if they are familiar with that particular text.

*Pragmatics*

A child's metareading knowledge of pragmatics can also be evaluated by the preschool teacher or interventionist by observing the child's behavior in various reading-related contexts. A structured task directed toward the child's awareness of author intent might require the child to indicate various types of books. For example, the teacher could direct the child to point to or otherwise indicate the book about animals, a princess, ABCs, or other types of children's books. Much of the child's ability to determine intent in this way will depend on the variety of books to which the child has been exposed. For example, if children have never experienced fairy tales or stories about a prince or princess, they naturally will be less able to designate correctly such a choice. Therefore, in addition to the child's pragmatic metareading awareness, the teacher will discover information relevant to the child's reading experiential background.

A setting in which the teacher or evaluator observes the child in spontaneous interaction with a book or other form of reading material may also be used to gather information concerning the child's knowledge of pragmatics at a metareading level. In this case, it is best to provide the child with a book that is a favorite story or one that is very familiar. Another alternative would be to allow the child to select a book from among several possibilities. As in the observation of the child to determine awareness of text cohesion, the child should be allowed to peruse the material with no intervention from adults. Data can be derived by recording and analyzing the verbalization and behavior that the child portrays during the time spent in "reading" the book. Attention should be directed to how well the child determines the intent of the author. For example, the book may reflect the author's purpose in telling about a horse that lives on a farm. Even a very young child may glean such intent from examination of the book. Utterances such as "here a horsey, horsey in barn," can provide clues to the observer that the child indeed knows what the story is about. The child's ability to detect and use old and new information markers can be observed. The utterance, "here horsey, he big," indicates by the use of pronominalization that the child understands that the topic need not be repeated because it has already been introduced and has become shared information.

Information about the child's awareness and knowledge of pragmatics at the level of metareading can also be derived by observing children as an adult reads to them. Interaction like requiring a child to retell parts of the story or episodes can present opportunities to detect the child's ability to determine author intent and old/new information markers. Turntaking can be observed by alternating character roles between reader and child.

## Semantics

The teacher or interventionist may also set a context in which to examine a child's metareading knowledge as it applies to semantics. Procedures that require the child to point to or locate proper names, topic words, or pertinent descriptors in the written text are helpful. This does not necessarily mean that the child will actually read the word, but rather that certain salient features, such as a capital letter at the beginning of the word, can clue the child to the word's referent. Asking the child to describe or label pictures in the story may demonstrate the richness or paucity of the child's vocabulary as well as the variety of underlying semantic cases or relationships.

As the child interacts with books unassisted by adults, several behaviors that provide clues to semantic understanding of the process of reading can be observed. The child who has had a story read several times will probably reiterate that story when reading the book. If the story has been read many times by a parent or teacher, the child's "reading" may actually be a form of recall or memorization of the story. In the early phases of this process, it is important for the teacher to observe which aspects of the story the child recalls, since this can be a clue to the developing schema associated with stories of various types. The child's retelling of the story should be expected to follow some of the known rules of story grammar (to be further delineated later in this book) and to include introduction of characters, goals, and episodes. Another behavior that would suggest growing knowledge of meaning in reading would be the child's reading or telling the story and explaining about reading to another child or even to a doll or toy animal.

The storyreading context may allow the child to verbalize or perform other types of behavior relating to semantics at a metareading level. For example, the child may pretend to act out the role of a story character and dramatize the episodes of the story. The child may involve the adult by requesting that the latter also portray a character or characters in the story. The observer should be alert to the child's interjections and inclusions of other stories that would indicate generalization of meaning across stories. A child might refer to a story about "Bossy the cow" as related to the story the child is listening to about the farm. In other words, the child is able to make generalizations or transfer aspects of schema and meaning across story boundaries. Further observation should include discussions of aspects of the story-reading context. Generalization might occur in spoken discourse as the child refers to a character or incident drawn from previous stories the child has heard.

*Syntax*

The assessment of syntax at the level of metareading knowledge may be accomplished as a controlled task in several ways. Many books present formats that employ repetition of a syntactic pattern ("The cat got on the bus." "The dog got on the bus." "The cow got on the bus." etc.). Such stories or books can be read to the child to determine if the child will pick up and carry through the application of the selected pattern by predicting what the next page will entail. In other words, the child's recognition and understanding of the syntactic pattern can be determined even though the child is not reading the words of the sentence per se.

Metareading syntactic information may also be derived from observation of children involved in book exploration on their own. Recording the verbalizations of the children as they examine the books or reading material will produce utterance samples that reflect how the children syntactically code the story information from what they are able to derive from pictures and other clues. Analysis of this type of information necessitates the teacher's familiarity with current syntactic analysis procedures. This type of syntactic procedure goes well beyond simple specification of numbers of nouns, verbs, and other parts of speech used by the child. It includes complete specification of the base structure and transformational system common to the English language as used by the child. This type of analysis requires a comprehensive understanding of the syntactic system and should not be lightly undertaken by the interventionist. If the story or book is familiar to the child, the sentences the child uses in restructuring the story will present similar information based on the understanding of the story that the child has internalized. These observations can also be made in an evaluation setting based on the adult reading to a child.

*Graphomorphophonemics*

Information about metareading at the GMP level may also be observed in the contexts or settings previously suggested. Metareading knowledge at this level includes distinguishing pictures, written symbols, words, letters, phoneme patterns, word boundaries, syllabification, and spelling patterns. Verbal play in spoken language and motor experimentation with pencils and crayons represent metareading associated with GMP. For example, graphic rehearsal can take the form of miscellaneous written "letters" that the child offers as an example of writing a story (this is addressed further in Chapter 7). As in the other instances of observation and evaluation of the psycho-socio-linguistic components as applied to metareading, it is important at the GMP level to view the child's behavior as a reflection of the child's current level of knowledge of reading rather than proficiency with a set of skills.

In evaluating within the GMP component, teachers or interventionists must go beyond the limited concerns that usually accompany assessment at this level. They must be concerned with more than just whether the child can recognize, match, or indicate beginning, medial, or final consonant sounds related to printed letters and words.

**Nonverbal and Low-Verbal Children**

The foregoing evaluation tasks assume a level of spoken language that allows the child to communicate a knowledge of metareading. Low-verbal children or children with little or no spoken language (hearing-impaired, severely language-disordered, and mentally retarded children) may not process or demonstrate metareading knowledge in the same manner as do children with more efficient use of the linguistic system. However, this does not mean that such children do not possess any knowledge concerning the reading process. For such children, many of the evaluation tasks can be modified in ways to allow for observation of metareading knowledge across all the language components discussed previously. Young, linguistically limited, hearing-impaired children, for example, may be unable to verbalize or retell stories, but they may demonstrate knowledge as to how one should posture in reading or how a book should be held. This is important metareading knowledge related to the activity of reading. Such information is helpful in conjunction with other associated data in designating the extent of current metareading knowledge that a child has and the extent of the child's potential risk for reading difficulty.

The following questions may serve as guides in the observation and evaluation of preschool children to determine their metareading knowledge. Deficits that appear should elicit concern for the child's future reading success. Consideration must be given to the nature of the deficit and the steps taken to alleviate or eliminate the indicated potential failure or difficulty.

- Is the child interested in books and other reading materials?
- Has the child been exposed to reading materials?
- Does the child's exposure include a variety of literature?
- Does the child understand the concepts related to reading (books, stories, etc.)?
- Does the child pretend to read?
- Does the child verbalize or vocalize in such pretending?
- Does the child attend to pictures?
- Does the child identify aspects of book format (beginning, end, title, etc.)?
- Does the child request written forms to represent spoken forms?
- Does the child attempt to restructure or retell stories?
- Does the child label story pictures as to characters or events in the story?
- Does the child describe pictures as related to the story sequence?
- Does the child relate other information to stories derived from related experiences?

## SPOKEN LANGUAGE AS AN INDICATOR OF POTENTIAL WRITTEN LANGUAGE DIFFICULTIES

To review, the linguistic components of the model presented in Chapter 3, as applied to written language, are:

- graphomorphophonemics
- syntax
- semantics
- pragmatics
- text cohesion

The counterparts of the first four of these components for spoken language would be:

- phonology
- syntax
- semantics
- pragmatics

By observing and analyzing a child's performance in these areas of spoken language, an "informal" evaluation of the child's state of readiness or knowledge of metareading can be carried out and applied to reading.

### Phonology

The development of spoken language can be used as a gauge for determining the intactness of the entire linguistic system. Through the observation and subsequent analysis of aspects of phonology, it is possible to predict the probable difficulties in reading that are related to the GMP component. The child who has phonological or articulatory disorders can be expected to have difficulty using such strategies in breaking the reading code via phonics, which is the commonly used initial instructional procedure in the teaching of beginning reading. The literature suggests a correlation between children's manifest problems in articulation and difficulties in learning to read.

These conclusions should be quite obvious. It should not surprise us that failure or difficulty occurs when instruction depends on the intact operation of a system or ability. For example, if the ability to ride a bicycle depends on a particular level of motor coordination, we should not be amazed if a child with severe cerebral palsy is unable to accomplish the task. The analogy with reading and problems in the area of phonology should be clear.

In addressing reading problems that involve the phonological component of language, we usually are concerned with the aspect of articulation or the expression component. It is also important to consider that the child's difficulty may occur within the receptive component or in conjunction with auditory processing decisions at the GMP level. Hasenstab and Schoeny (1981) point out that auditory processing is not a set of discrete skills but a series of decisions made on incoming auditory information by the auditory system. A child may appear to have a problem at the GMP level as related to auditory memory when in fact the child is unable to make processing decisions at the earlier levels of selected attention or stimuli differentiation.

Because the linguistic subsystems are interrelated, a difficulty in one of them often signals disruption in some or all of the other subsystems as well. Articulation, an aspect of the phonological subsystem in spoken language, may indicate disruption in syntactic, semantic, and/or pragmatic subsystems of the written language as well. Articulation and evidence of auditory processing problems may be the first indications of potential reading difficulty.

### Syntax

If a child exhibits problems in the area of articulation, further evaluation should assess the child's facility in the subsystem of syntax. However, even if the phonological operation appears to be intact, this is no guarantee that the child will not demonstrate restrictions at the level of syntax. Therefore, observation of linguistic performance must also include evaluation of the child's use of syntax in spontaneous spoken language. Speech that is characterized by lack of syntactic flexibility or by the use of short basic sentences with no attempt to change, transform, elaborate, or modify should alert the astute observer to a potential reading problem.

In relating the syntax of spoken language to syntactic concerns in reading, it should be apparent that a child will be unable to process information presented at a written syntactic level that is not commensurate with the child's overall syntactic level of ability. In view of the fact that there is a high level of syntactic complexity in most early basal reading series, teachers and other professionals concerned with success in reading must be attuned to this fact.

### Semantics

Warning signals of possible problems in children's reading proficiency that are cued by the linguistic subsystem of semantics may be even more subtle than those cued by phonology or syntax in spoken language. Clues to semantically related problems might include restricted vocabulary development and use, difficulty of comprehension of spoken language, and difficulties in formulating spoken language. Problems in comprehension of spoken language are based on difficulties in the intact functioning of the auditory system. Auditory processing disorders that affect decisions made at semantic level are at a more sophisticated level than those involved in GMP strategies.

Decisions made in the processing of auditory information as to meaningful versus nonmeaningful and linguistic versus nonlinguistic auditory stimuli are semantically based (Hasenstab & Schoeny, 1982; Sanders,

1982). An internal semantic representation of the stimulus must be present in order for such decisions to be made. This type of problem might manifest itself in a child finding it difficult or being unable to follow directions, answer questions correctly, or understand connected discourse.

Formulation problems may be evidenced by a child's inability to sequence ideas into a logical retelling of events or activities. They may also manifest in a child's inability to describe occurrences or actions, to communicate effectively desires or needs, or to employ semantic variations in interactions with others.

Restricted vocabulary refers not only to a limitation in the number of words that a child uses but also to limitations in the variation of the type of roles or cases that the child assigns to words. For example, a child may appear to have a large vocabulary. However, close examination of the child's repertoire may reveal that the words used are primarily nouns applied as agents with little other development of the verb system or semantic cases.

In addition, semantic analysis calls for examination of conceptual understanding beyond vocabulary; that is, does the child understand and use relational terms, as in prepositions? The quality of schema representation is also covered in this area, extending beyond the mere recognition of verbal symbols as representing concepts. The extent of a child's schematic understanding of objects, events, and actions is a valuable foundation for context that is so vital to adequate comprehension in reading.

Semantic delay or deficiency in spoken language affecting vocabulary, comprehension, and production may suggest a potential for semantically induced reading problems. Thus, it is imperative that examination of a child's language performance be extended beyond phonological and syntactical levels to the more subtle semantic indicators of linguistic limitation.

## Pragmatics

Early predictors of reading problems that arise from a lack of facility in the pragmatic uses of language may present themselves in several forms. Normally developing children learn very early how to use language for social purposes. Halliday (1975) has described the following functions of language:

| | |
|---|---|
| Instrumental | I want |
| Regulatory | Do as I tell you |
| Interactional | Me and you |
| Personal | Here I come |

| Heuristic | Tell me why |
| Imaginative | Let's pretend |
| Informative | I've got something to tell you (p. 6) |

Children who are described as shy may have little functional use of language to effect social change in their immediate environments. They do not understand the power of language in gaining their wants and desires or in persuading, and they may be unable to use language for these purposes.

## POSSIBLE HIGH-RISK INDICATORS RELATED TO SPOKEN LANGUAGE

The following high-risk indicators related to spoken language at the four component levels of phonology, syntax, semantics, and pragmatics may alert the interventionist, teacher, or other evaluator to the potential for reading problems. It must be remembered that the appearance or evidence of one indicator may not by itself signal a probable reading difficulty. It does, however, suggest that the child should be observed carefully. Observation of several high-risk indicators should signal the need for intervention at the subsystem level indicated. All of these indicators are assumed to be outside what is considered to be age-appropriate development.

1. Phonology

   - developmental delay in articulation acquisition
   - multiple omission, substitutions, and distortions in speech sound production
   - poor intelligibility of speech
   - disruption in prosody
   - difficulty in sound orientation
   - problems in selective auditory attention
   - problems in sustained auditory attention
   - inability to determine nature of sound (human vs. environmental)

2. Syntax

   - use of restricted forms in sentences
   - use of ungrammatical forms
   - overuse of short basic sentences
   - limited application of transformations
   - lack of appropriate pronoun use
   - limited variety of sentence forms
   - misapplication of articles, deictic forms
   - inability to sequence information (auditory)

3. Semantics

- limited vocabulary
- narrow use of semantic cases
- failure to understand verbal directions
- failure to understand discourse
- limited concept development
- underdeveloped schema
- inability to synthesize auditory information

4. Pragmatics

- failure to communicate intent
- inability to follow turntaking routines
- failure to cue the listener to the topic of discussion
- failure to use clarification strategies when misunderstood
- overdependence on performatives
- inability in comprehending and communicating old and new information

## SUMMARY

The intent of this chapter was to indicate some ways in which preschool teachers, interventionists, or other professionals charged with the evaluation and education of young children might identify via "informal" observation, children who are probably at-risk candidates for later reading difficulties. Since reading is a linguistic process, evaluation, whether formal or informal, should result from a language-oriented foundation. Therefore, observation and analysis must be based on examination of the child's performance with respect to the psycho-socio-linguistic components related to both the child's spoken language facility and knowledge at the level of metareading.

# Chapter 5

# Reading Evaluation and Reading Disabilities

*W* ho was under the spell of a wicked old witch . . .

## DIAGNOSTIC EVALUATION

Evaluation in reading has traditionally involved two primary purposes: diagnosis of a reading problem and measurement of reading aptitude or ability. Diagnostic testing in reading attempts to describe or verify the presence and/or extent of a reading disability. As Salvia and Ysseldyke (1978, 1981) emphasize, evaluation consequently provides teachers with data that will assist in the development of strengths and the remediation of weaknesses. Whether or not diagnostic reading instruments satisfactorily achieve this objective is currently an issue of debate.

### General Description of Diagnostic Reading Tests

Although there has been some attempt to use criterion-referenced tests, at the present time most reading tests that are diagnostic in nature are norm referenced and designed to compare an individual student's reading ability with that of peers as represented by a normed population. Resulting performance is expressed in scores related to grade levels, percentile ranks, or stanines for various aspects measured by the instrument. Although diagnostic reading instruments are considered to be standardized tests, they vary greatly as to technical adequacy and have been criticized because of a "relative lack of reliability and the absence of empirical evidence for their validity" (Salvia and Ysseldyke, 1978, p. 164). Diagnostic reading tests are usually individualized tests, administered to a single child by an examiner rather than within a classroom or to a small group of students. However, some tests that are diagnostic and norm referenced in nature are designed to be used with groups of students and administered by teachers. These are sometimes referred to as reading survey tests.

Tests designed as diagnostic reading instruments present items, subtests, or components to evaluate a broad spectrum of reading and reading-related skills. The tests vary in composition, depending on the author's definition of the reading process and what aspects are determined to be pertinent to reading ability and performance. Generally, however, diagnostic evaluation examines oral reading ability, word analysis or word attack skills, word recognition, reading rate, and, in some way, word, sentence, or paragraph understanding.

## Skills Evaluated

### Oral Reading

Traditionally, oral reading ability has been considered to be an extremely important facility to be mastered by a reader. In most cases, diagnostic tests of reading address this skill as a subtest in which passages are arranged in graduated order of difficulty. The student is required to read the material aloud, and the examiner records test-specific errors made by the reader during the reading. In many cases, behaviors are also noted, such as finger pointing and frequent loss of place. In addition to oral reading subtests that are components of diagnostic test batteries, there are also reading evaluation instruments that concentrate wholly on the measurement of oral reading ability. (See Appendix A for summaries of diagnostic reading tests.)

The types of oral reading errors or behaviors that diagnostic tests focus upon vary from test to test. Salvia and Ysseldyke (1978, 1981), however, cite 10 types of errors that are covered in various reading tests.

1. Aid. The examiner is required to pronounce the word for the reader. Error is recorded by an underlined bracket.
2. Gross mispronunciation. Pronunciation that varies greatly from the actual word presented. Error is recorded by phonetically writing above the word.
3. Omission. A word or group of words is skipped by the reader. Error is recorded by circling omitted words.
4. Insertion. The addition of words to a reading passage. Error is designated by a carat (ʌ) and words recorded.
5. Repetition. Repeating of words or groups of words. The repeated words are underlined with a wavy line.
6. Substitution. Replacement of words or groups of words. Errors are recorded by underlining and writing in of substituted words.
7. Inversion. Changes in sentence word order. Errors are indicated as in "‌boy‌tall‌."

8. Partial mispronunciation. Only a part of a word is mispronounced. Errors are recorded phonetically.
9. Disregard for punctuation. Failure to observe punctuation by pause or intonation pattern as required. Error is recorded by circling the punctuation mark.
10. Hesitation. A pause of 2 or more seconds before a word is pronounced. Error is indicated by a check ($\checkmark$) over the word.

### *Word Analysis or Word Attack Skills*

Several tests have been developed as diagnostic evaluation instruments that specialize in word analysis. Because the view has persisted that words cannot be understood unless they can be pronounced or recoded to their auditory representation (see Chapter 2), some reading tests include subtests directed toward the evaluation of word analysis or word attack skills. Reading evaluation may include the analysis of letter-sound associations and the identification of vowels, consonants or consonant clusters, and rules of syllabication and sound blending. Heilman (1968) categorizes word analysis skills in five main groups. The inclusion of a specific skill evaluation, however, ultimately depends on the test author's definition of reading-related skills. Heilman's five groups are:

1. word form—awareness of specific word configurations
2. structural analysis—knowledge of root words, prefixes, and suffixes
3. contextual clues—ability to analyze words through context of other words in a sentence or passage
4. picture clues—analysis of words by help of associated pictures
5. phonetic or phonic analysis—association of sounds with printed symbols

### *Word Recognition*

Most diagnostic reading tests include a subtest designed to assess a student's ability to recognize and pronounce words. This skill relates to an individual's "sight vocabulary," which is comprised of words that the reader need not employ word attack strategies on in order to determine oral representation. Word recognition tests actually examine how well a student can translate a visual representation to an auditory/vocal representation or symbol. They concern the recoding of graphemic rules to phonological rules and also involve one's ability to blend sounds, determine syllable boundaries, and apply suprasegmental emphasis at the word level. Internalization of visual representation for auditory/vocal ability is not always obvious, and word recognition does not guarantee comprehension of word meaning. Generally word recognition tests are components of a larger test battery.

*Reading Rate*

Compared to other areas addressed, rate of reading receives relatively little attention in diagnostic reading tests. Reading rate is usually concerned with a student's ability to read rapidly material that is familiar and relatively easy. This is perhaps one area in which traditional evaluation approaches are actually of value in determining proficient readers. However, the method of evaluation and the failure to examine the ability to vary the rate for different types of reading material usually results in the test falling short of adequate assessment of this ability.

*Comprehension in Reading*

Generally, diagnostic reading tests contain one or more components that examine comprehension in some form. Many attempt to evaluate passage comprehension along three dimensions: literal comprehension, or information directly presented in the passage; inferential comprehension, which requires interpretation based on printed information; and listening comprehension, which requires recall after listening to a passage read aloud by the examiner. In most cases, these levels of comprehension are examined through the presentation of questions, either orally or in printed form. If children answer the questions correctly, it is assumed that they understood what they read or heard read to them. However, if the children do not answer the questions correctly, it cannot be presumed that they do not understand the material. They may not understand the question. The ability to answer questions, either printed or spoken, or to recall information presented as auditory stimuli is a complex function that is in most instances totally ignored by existing diagnostic reading tests in the evaluation of comprehension.

Tests designed to evaluate reading comprehension may take various forms. For children at early reading stages, comprehension of sentences may be included in reading evaluation. This usually involves a task such as matching a sentence to a picture by drawing a line or by pointing as appropriate. Another form requires children to select a correct word from a multiple choice set that will make a sentence relate to a picture. Word comprehension may be a task included for both early readers and readers at higher levels. Format naturally varies depending on the age and ability levels of the students evaluated. Definitions may be requested, synonyms matched, words requested by analogous presentation, or words matched to pictures depicting word meaning.

Tests of reading comprehension may also be used as independent evaluation tools rather than as components of a larger test battery. These tests may examine comprehension either by an oral reading format or a silent reading approach; they might include oral and written questions, cloze procedures, or definitions.

Tuinman (1973) questions exactly what it is that tests claiming to evaluate reading comprehension actually measure. In his evaluation of five major testing instruments, he concludes that the tests lack controls to ensure that correct answering of a particular comprehension item was due to reading a selected passage. The issue of format for assessing comprehension is clearly one that should concern the teacher and evaluator; it raises the question as to whether comprehension is examined at all.

## TYPES OF READING EVALUATION TESTS

### Tests of Achievement

Achievement testing, which may take the form of a screening device or an in-depth examination, is employed primarily to determine reading performance based on a particular grade level. Evaluation of reading performance or reading achievement focuses on the student's mastery of specific reading "skills" as related to defined levels or other criteria of accomplishment. Results of testing show areas or skills that have been "learned" and indicate those abilities that have not yet been mastered. Tests of reading achievement may be formal standardized instruments, informal commercially made tests, or informal teacher-designed materials.

Currently, commercially prepared achievement tests of a battery design, with a subtest or subtests that examine reading ability or skills, enjoy the greatest popularity. Figure 5–1 lists the most commonly used commercial achievement batteries. In most cases, the reading components address vocabulary via word recognition tasks or a general comprehension of words, sentences, or short passages. Since the purpose of general achievement tests is to ascertain overall academic functioning of a student, it is not within their domain to attempt in-depth assessment of reading.

Karlin (1971) suggests that information resulting from general achievement tests may be helpful in identifying students who require more in-depth evaluation in reading. Therefore, achievement batteries may serve as useful screening devices in reading. In actuality, however, caution must be exercised in placing much trust either in the global reading scores achieved by totaling several reading subtests to obtain grade equivalent scores or in the grade equivalents that are represented by the performance of one "reading" task, such as word recognition.

**Figure 5–1** Achievement Tests with Reading Subtests

| Test | Areas Evaluated |
|------|-----------------|
| Comprehensive Test of Basic Skills (CTBS). E. Tiegs & W. Clarke. Monterey, Cal.: McGraw-Hill (1968, revised 1970). | Reading vocabulary<br>Reading comprehension |
| Metropolitan Achievement Test (MAT). B. Balow, H. Bixler, W. Durost, G. Prescott, & J. Wrightstone. New York: Harcourt, Brace, Jovanovich (1970). | Reading vocabulary<br>Word analysis<br>Reading comprehension |
| Peabody Individual Achievement Test (PIAT). L. Dunn & F. Markwardt. Circle Pines, Minn.: American Guidance Service (1970). | Reading vocabulary |
| Wide Range Achievement Test (WRAT). J. Jastak, S. Kijou, & S. Jostak. Wilmington, Del.: Guidance Associates of Delaware (1973, revised 1975). | Reading vocabulary |
| SRA Achievement Series. R. A. Naslund, L. P. Thorpe, & D. W. Lefever. Chicago: Science Research Associates (1954, revised 1958, 1963, 1978). | Word-picture association<br>Reading vocabulary<br>Reading comprehension |
| Woodcock-Johnson Psychoeducational Battery: Tests of Achievement. R. Woodcock & M. Johnson. Hingham, Maine: Teaching Resources Corp. (1977). | Reading vocabulary<br>Reading comprehension<br>Word analysis |

**Other Forms of Reading Evaluation**

We have seen that tests designed for diagnostic evaluation in reading are used to determine areas of difficulty (and strength) related to a student's progress in learning to read. Achievement testing specifically related to reading is used to determine reading performance as compared to other students of the same age or grade. Reading ability is also observed or actually scored as a subtest component in tests of intelligence and in general achievement tests designed to evaluate skill development in several subject areas.

In addition to published tests, which have received primary emphasis in this section, informal types of reading evaluation are also used to examine aspects of oral and silent reading, word analysis skills, and word recognition. Teachers or clinicians involved in the task of teaching either developmental or remedial reading may also employ informal reading inventories, which can provide helpful information in specific reading areas; observation of the student's reading behavior and performance; and teacher-designed tests, which often meet particular situational needs more appropriately than standardized instruments.

**Criterion-Referenced Tests**

Criterion-referenced tests, like standardized reading tests, are designed to examine a student's strengths and weaknesses in reading. They are unique, however, in that their purpose is not to compare performance with other readers of the same age, grade, and so on, but to provide information that may be used as the basis for a reading instruction program. In other words, they provide a task analysis of reading behaviors. The individual child's performance or ability may be examined in relation to criteria that are designated as specific to the child's program needs. The criteria may change from one student to another, thereby theoretically allowing greater flexibility, individualization, and experiential activities for students. This flexibility is especially appealing when addressing children with handicapping conditions that affect growth in reading development, such as students who may be hearing impaired or mentally retarded or who may display language difficulties due to other circumstances.

*Advantages*

Criterion-referenced tests offer several advantages over standardized testing procedures in providing the basis for the development of objectives for reading instruction. Proger and Mann (1973) cite four such advantages. The first relates to the flexibility for individual students, which, as we have noted, is a definite asset. The second advantage, closely related to the first, is the fact that such testing judges children's performances relative to their own abilities or deficiencies. A third advantage is that criterion-referenced testing permits a process of ongoing evaluation to determine progress. The fourth advantage is the adaptability of criterion-referenced tests to commercial reading programs.

*Some Difficulties*

Despite these advantages, there are some cautionary notes regarding the use of criterion-referenced tests. Hallahan and Kaufman (1976) indicate that one problem exists in the selection of appropriate criteria that are neither too easy nor too difficult. Another potential difficulty arises from the fact that criterion-referenced tests vary both in the targeted skills and the sequences in which the skills are presented. As with standardized tests, what a particular author includes in an evaluation instrument is based on that author's fundamental definition of reading. Thus, criterion-referenced tests may be centered on the same auditory and visual skills that are basic to standardized tests yet avoid a more linguistically oriented emphasis. Salvia and Ysseldyke (1978) cite an additional concern in the use of criterion-referenced evaluation, that of reliability. They emphasize that reliability is important in this form of evaluation because of the concern for consistent responses to test items. "If a different pattern of item scores is obtained each time an individual takes the test, we begin to question the reliability of the device" (Salvia & Ysseldyke, 1981, p. 218). They stress that test authors should report test-retest reliabilities for test items and alternate forms of reliability data when more than one form of a test is available for use.

Criterion-referenced testing indeed presents several advantages in reading evaluation oriented toward the individual student. Nevertheless, the teacher must still pay close attention to the underlying definition of reading upon which the test is designed, to the appropriateness of the specific criteria for particular students, and to the reliability of the test.

**Summary**

There are several levels of reading evaluation available to the teacher or clinician addressing reading instruction and/or intervention with school-aged students. Yet individual instruments may or may not adequately evaluate what they purport to evaluate. Some standardized instruments provide appropriate normative information and acceptable reliability and validity data, while others do not. Informal commercial tests and classroom-centered evaluation may examine the skill areas examined in this section. However, the question is whether such evaluation deals with reading as it relates to language. The assessment approach of the tests we have examined defines reading as a set of skills, both auditory and visual, that must be mastered before a student can successfully read. Yet, although such skills are of value and are accomplished by proficient readers, their evaluation does not assess the underlying foundation of reading, which is linguistic in nature, not skill oriented.

## PROBLEMS CONCERNING CURRENT EVALUATION IN READING

The central concern in reading evaluation is not the issue of whether reading tests, diagnostic or achievement oriented, actually measure the skills and abilities that they define and claim to measure. Of greater importance is the question of whether the targeted skills or abilities are, in fact, indicators of reading facility related to the child's linguistic system. F. Smith (1973) states that tests of reading measure only "facility in an assortment of drills, rules and power tasks that at best bear only a tangential relation to fluent reading" (p. 191). He adds that the failure of reading tests to assess reading ability accurately is due to the misconceptions in the test design concerning the nature of reading. Inaccurate definitions and faulty underlying premises produce inaccurate and inappropriate evaluation instruments.

Goldberg and Schiffman (1972) provide evidence of further difficulty. One of the major barriers in the identification of reading disabilities is the dependence of professionals on the results of standardized testing instruments, which, because they are based on a "frustration level," do not accurately indicate the optimal level for a student's instruction. These authors state that no single test can measure the aspect of reading as it relates to language.

The content of standardized tests is also an area of problematic concern. King (1977) notes that the content or selection of evaluation items that are removed from the context of reality may be highly boring to the child being tested, or at least be limited in an ability to motivate the child's best performance. If we are concerned that the evaluation must be a measure of ability, it is important that the child we are testing at least be somewhat interested in the task at hand.

As noted previously, Salvia and Ysseldyke (1981) maintain that standardized reading evaluation also suffers from a technical standpoint. Some existing tests, although they may include elaborate normative tables for the interpretation of test results, fail to define clearly the normative population on which the tables were based.

The gradually increasing use of criterion-referenced instruments represents a less rigid approach to testing and may definitely pose some advantages. It is, however, still too early to make such a determination. Thus, caution must be exercised regarding test content and the definition of reading upon which the criteria are developed. If the ''skill'' orientation persists, we continue to observe aspects of performance that do not represent or indicate reading function or ability. It is not just the construction of a test that makes it a viable measure, but also the underlying philosophical position upon which it is based. No matter how well a test is designed, if its users do not view reading accurately, it cannot assess the ability to master the function.

The difficulties with reading evaluation as it exists in general practice today are indeed alarming, since inaccurate or inappropriate testing, which is the basis for subsequent instruction, can actually undermine the successful accomplishment of reading for some children. In addition to the concerns we have presented, King (1977) cites four additional limitations of existing tests. She charges that they are: ''biased in favor of children from middle class homes where standard English is spoken; partial to the experience, style of speech, and values of middle class homes; biased toward children who mature early in verbal skills and follow rather conventional thinking patterns; give advantage to children who have experienced certain traditional teaching methods and penalizes those who have learned in more divergent ways'' (p. 408).

## READING DISABILITY

### Historical Overview

As early as 1877, Kussmaul noted a condition in which an individual was unable to interpret written form in spite of the fact that he demonstrated adequate intelligence, speech and visual acuity. Kussmaul termed the condition *word blindness*. Morgan (1896) reported the case of a young boy, also of normal intelligence, speech, and vision, who could not read or spell anything other than very simple words. The central characteristic of the condition was normal vision but an inability to interpret printed or written language. The term that replaced Kussmaul's description was *dyslexia,* which means quite simply an inability to recognize letters or words.

Orton (1937) has described dyslexic children as exhibiting the following characteristics:

- reading ability lagging behind development in other areas
- tendency to reverse letters and words
- facility for mirror reading

Orton was struck by the frequency of reversals, and thus another term related to reading difficulty emerged. Orton's term for this is *strephosymbolica,* meaning twisted symbol.

The observation of children who are unable to master reading has continued to the present time. Various terminologies, ideas on etiology, approaches for evaluation and remediation, and ways of developing materials have come into vogue and met with varying degrees of success and failure. As yet, however, we have not solved the problem of reading disability.

**Causes of Reading Disability**

Despite evaluation instrumentation, special education programs specifically designed for the remediation of reading problems, and a wealth of commercially available reading materials, reading disabilities remain as the greatest source of school failure (Strang, 1969). As Wallace and Larsen (1978) indicate, various reasons have been advanced and discussed to account for the existence of such problems in children. A medical or pathological point of view is based on a dysfunction of the brain, which then results in an inability to interpret written information. Teaching techniques, instructional materials, and factors related to educational environment and experiences have also been linked to limited success in learning to read. Difficulties in visual and auditory processing, without observable pathology, are other cited reasons for failure in reading mastery. Early research by Robinson (1946) suggests that in fact there is a multiplicity of factors that affect reading success, related to the individual child's physiological, psychological, societal, educational, and environmental circumstances.

The issue of etiology is addressed by Weiner and Cromer (1967) in their description of four models that may account for reading disability or reading failure. These models are similar to those identified by other researchers.

1. the defect model, which attributes failure in reading to organic difficulty
2. the deficit model, which assumes a deficiency in reading skills
3. the disruption model, which suggests atypical function in learning
4. the difference model, which implies a variation of linguistic code

In elaboration of these classifications, Gormley and Franzen (1978) explain that the defect model assumes that a problem such as a learning disability, the presence of a hearing loss, or mental retardation prohibits reading development. The deficit model assumes that children with handicapping conditions do not have the necessary phonological, syntactic, semantic, or pragmatic information for successful mastery in reading; that is, a language deficit is the basis of the reading disability. In the disruption model, the causes stem from a source of interruption in the acquisition of language or the development of reading ability. Finally, in the difference model, Gormley and Franzen assume a mismatch between the child's "native" language and the method of instruction, as in bilingualism or in the case of hearing-impaired children who use a manual communication system that is not based in English syntax. The difference model does not consider oral language competence as a prerequisite to reading. It suggests that the major problem is in a language variation or difference.

The actual etiology of reading disability is still a subject of much conjecture. Poor muscular function of the eyes, lack of cerebral dominance, heredity, blood diseases, and improper glandular function have all been cited as causes. However, to date, none of these has been thoroughly substantiated.

Although each suggested etiology for the existence of reading disability is plausible and defendable, one factor has been consistently ignored in consideration of a failure to read. This is the fact that reading is language. It is with this orientation that many answers might be found to help solve the many mysteries of reading disability.

**Definitions**

The difficulties related to the mastery of reading are addressed by several disciplines, including education, psychology, and medicine. We have seen that, historically, several terms have been applied in an attempt to define the phenomenon. A variety of terms has continued to emerge from various disciplines, each focusing on a particular point of view. The nomenclature includes such terms as dyslexia, reading disorder, reading disability, specific developmental dyslexia, congenital word blindness, specific reading disability, and developmental lag in reading (Goldberg and Schiffman, 1972).

Goldberg and Schiffman (1972) suggest two definitive categories of children with reading problems. The first, termed *primary reading retardation*, is characterized by obvious brain damage. This would occur, for example, in the case of a child with cerebral palsy or "a basic incapacity to integrate or interpret written material and to associate concepts or symbols" (p. 17). This may be the result of central trauma, metabolic imbalance, or problems related to the development of the brain and central nervous system. *Secondary reading retardation* refers to children with reading delay due to external causes, such as education or environmental detriments. These two basic categories have been quite popular in the classification of reading disabilities. They can also be seen to be related closely to the etiology models proposed by Weiner and Cromer (1967).

## LANGUAGE AS A BASIS FOR READING EVALUATION

### Evaluation Strategies

In assessing the strategies of readers, Clay (1968) found that children usually guess at points of uncertainty in their reading. She suggests that such guessing is determined by mastery or control of syntax by the reader. She posits that, by the time of entry in school, the child who reads successfully will have generally mastered the level of syntactic ability necessary for guessing or hypothesizing strategies. At beginning of reading instruction, the child thus possesses some control in reading and hence in the academic areas related to reading.

To update Clay's observations concerning syntax, we must include semantic and pragmatic knowledge as well as text cohesion and story format. This additional knowledge is also brought by the child to the reading activity. The quality and quantity of each component will, however, vary from child to child. In the observation and evaluation of reading from a linguistic point of view, it is important to determine a child's strategy for dealing with printed information.

### Paraphrasing and Recall

Paraphrase may be defined as a restatement of text, paragraph, or sentence wherein the meaning of the original form remains intact but the surface structure is altered. The activity of paraphrasing is actually a common linguistic function employed by language users in day-to-day communication. Seldom do we relate verbatim, or exactly how we initially read or heard, information previously acquired. Liberman, Mattingly, and Turvey (1972) emphasize that, except for cases requiring rote memory of information or immediate memory-span forms of information, recall takes the form of paraphrase. Restatement or paraphrase is therefore considered an essential condition in normal communication and memory of linguistic information. In fact, restructuring may be a necessity if information is to be stored and remembered over time.

Paraphrase may be said to be one of the best indications of comprehension (Salvia & Ysseldyke, 1981), depending on how one sees paraphrase as related to memory. If rote recall is the criterion, paraphrase would entail a certain degree of error. The aspects of the original message that remain intact may be seen as residual, unaffected by the process of for-getting. In this view, paraphrase may be seen as recall failure. However, paraphrase may also reflect a necessary condition that allows us to com-municate as well as remember. The efficiency and economy of language may actually depend on the phenomenon of paraphrase.

### Sentence Comprehension and Paraphrase

Kamm (1979) views sentence comprehension as an integral part of the reading process. Referring to such ability as a strand of sentence meaning skills, Kamm presents two aspects: one of analysis, focusing on passage specifics and detail, the other of synthesis, oriented toward paraphrase or restatement of meaning.

Effective comprehension of a sentence can be demonstrated by restate-ment in an equally meaningful way but by variation of the form. For example, paraphrase can occur by rearranging word order, substituting words, transforming sentences, and so on. However, the meaning or "gist" remains intact. The ability to paraphrase relates to the recognition of meaning equivalence between two propositions. Although syntactic or surface structure may change, as in, "Harvey baked the cookies," and, "The cookies were baked by Harvey," the underlying meaning or deep structure remains constant. The two propositions are actually paraphrases of one another.

To use paraphrase as an evaluation procedure, the reader is directed to retell a story just read. Analysis is then based on paraphrase information related to story events, representation of characters, story theme and plot, and major passage ideas or concepts. With such information as evidence, paraphrase or recall may be viewed as a feasible approach to a linguistic-based evaluation of reading. In order to glean meaning and present a recalled form of a passage, the reader must utilize the linguistic strategies available.

### Reading Miscues

The use of miscues in reading has been suggested and used by various researchers as a method of evaluation in reading (Burke & Goodman, 1970; Carlson, 1975; DeLawter, 1975; K. Goodman, 1967, 1969; Y. Good-man, 1970; Lipton, 1972; Nurss, 1969; Wardbaugh, 1969; Weaver, 1980; Zintz, 1980).

Reading miscues are assumed to be a natural and therefore expected occurrence in the reading process. Rather than errors in reading, they are viewed as rule misapplications that are explainable because they are rule governed, principled, and may be tied to a motivational base. As Zutell (1977) points out, even proficient readers demonstrate miscues. This may be due to the fact that "total accuracy [is sacrificed] for speed and efficiency" (p. 385). In addition, miscues have been noted as similar in occurrence for various kinds of reading content (Carlson, 1975). By using miscue analysis in reading evaluation, the evaluator may gain information concerning the strategies imposed by the child in an approach to written language.

In using reading miscues in evaluation, Y. Goodman (1970) explains that the miscue itself is not the central focus. Rather it is the quality or type of miscue that suggests reading strategy. Types of miscues vary with accomplished and beginning readers (Y. Goodman & Burke, 1972), with fluent and poor readers (K. Goodman & Burke, 1973; Weber, 1970), and also as a function of the reading approach used in instruction (Cohen, 1975; DeLawter, 1975).

Noting and analyzing miscues that occur in a child's reading may help to accomplish many of the evaluation goals we presently attempt to achieve through the use of standardized instruments. For example, consider the aspect of word recognition. As noted previously, word recognition has been included as a major component in reading testing. In most instances, the means for acquiring this type of information is through the use of word lists. Children read words, and their correct pronunciation is determined to indicate word knowledge. In studies by K. Goodman (1965), children's ability to recognize words was compared when the words were presented in isolation, as in word list form, and when the words were presented in context. He concluded that children were better able to recognize words in a meaningful context of a sentence or text. Since the goal of reading is comprehension, perhaps a more realistic approach to determine if a child can recognize words is the use of context. As Zintz (1980) points out, if we place emphasis on the extraction of meaning rather than on the correct articulation of the word, we might have fewer problems in learning to read.

The Reading Miscue Inventory (RMI), developed by Y. Goodman and Burke (1972), can be used as a procedure for evaluating reading comprehension. With this inventory, children are directed to read a story out loud. Scoring is based on the observer's noted variations from actual text representation.

Studies by Burke and Goodman (1970) in examining types of miscues indicate that some miscue forms do not result in change of meaning. In other words, the semanticity of the passage remains intact. An example of this type of miscue would be substitution of the word *woods* for *forest* in the sentence *Goldilocks went for a long walk in the forest*. Other types of semantic miscues can relate to dialect or colloquial differences in word use. Since readers first reconstruct meaning from the printed page before they recode to the aural/oral modality of code, they apply words that represent their own language experience.

Further studies illustrate that miscues are more apt to be corrected if meaning is affected or if the resulting syntax is unacceptable. Clay's (1968) examination of reading errors and self-correction as related to syntax indicates that there is dependence on the awareness that all words will not automatically or meaningfully fit together. A reader expects written information to fit the language structure that is familiar. With this knowledge in mind, the reader can determine that something is incongruent in the message.

Although we do not wish to imply that miscue analysis is the "end all" in reading evaluation, such analysis is helpful in gaining pertinent information regarding strategies (such as bottom-up or top-down processing) employed by the reader to attain comprehension. It can further assist in determining if suspected reading problems are indeed present or if the reader is, in fact, displaying only surface variations rather than errors in the reading process. Miscue analysis can also inform the teacher/evaluator of the correction strategies a child uses and which miscues are selected for correction.

There is a core of helpful and explanatory information available in the literature that the evaluator and teacher can peruse and utilize to advantage. For example, in addition to examining the RMI of Y. Goodman and Burke, we suggest reading Weaver's (1980) treatment of miscues. Miscue analysis in conjunction with other psycholinguistically based testing procedures can provide useful information that can be used to develop and implement an appropriate reading program.

## EVALUATION OF READING BASED ON THE MODEL

If we adopt a definition of reading that is based in psycho-socio-linguistic theory, then we must likewise adopt a procedure for evaluation based on such theory. By being cognizant of the psycho-socio-linguistic components of the model, the evaluator can assess in systematic fashion a student's reading accomplishment. The techniques procedures we have described, such as recall, paraphrase, and miscue analysis, can be valuable tools in assessment operations.

As may be evident from the discussion thus far, there is a paucity of formalized or standardized evaluation instruments designed to assess reading as we have defined it. However, it is possible to use some of the existing measures to determine performance in the various psycho-socio-linguistic aspects described in the model presented in Chapter 3. These existing measures can then be supplemented by criterion-referenced tests, which may need to be developed specifically by the evaluator or teacher. A thorough understanding of the psycho-sociolinguistic components, of the various constraints and strategies associated with them, and of their mutual interaction should provide the practitioner with the foundation upon which criteria for reading evaluation can be selected and developed.

**Text Cohesion and Pragmatics**

Although we are presently attempting to develop procedures for evaluating text cohesion and pragmatics in reading, there is no such procedure available at this time. The best approach therefore appears to be through the gathering, examination, and analysis of written language samples. The following questions may serve as guidelines to the evaluation of text cohesion and pragmatics in reading through the use of children's written samples.

- Is there a title?
- Does the title provide context for the story?
- Does the initial sentence(s) cue to the type of format used?
- What is the format of the text (story, poem, essay, etc.)?
- Is the format consistent throughout the text?
- Is the text written in paragraph form (unless it is poetry)?
- Do the sentences within the paragraphs tie together?
- What strategies does the writer use to tie the sentences together?
- How does the writer code old and new information (pronominalization, tense consistency, etc.)?
- Does the writer prioritize information?
- How does the writer prioritize information (relative clause, subordinate clause, etc.)?
- Is the author's intent obvious?

In addition to the evaluation of pragmatics and text cohesion through written language sample analyses, teacher observation of a child's attention to aspects of these psycho-socio-linguistic components in a reading activity can reveal helpful information. Questions, geared to the child's language level, might include:

- What does the title tell you about the story?
- What kind of format did the author use?
- What is the author trying to communicate to you?
- What is the topic (new information)?
- What contextual clues are provided by the pictures?

## Semantics

Semantics can be examined in several different ways. We have already mentioned miscue analysis, paraphrase, and story recall and reconstruction. The vocabulary aspects of semantics is an easily assessed area. The assessment can be carried out informally through the use of definitions, matching pictures to words or sentences, and so on. The evaluator should select a procedure of semantic evaluation that is appropriate to the child's developmental age and interest level.

In assessing semantics as related to a broad meaning perspective, in addition to using paraphrase and story recall, evaluators and/or teachers might address the following questions:

- Can the child determine the underlying idea or meaning of the passage?
- Based on the passage format, can the child determine the appropriate elements (story setting, problem, resolution)?
- Can the child infer information not specifically stated in the text?
- Does the child's comprehension extend beyond individual word meaning?
- Does the child comprehend the author's use of cataphoric and anaphoric reference?
- Does the child have sufficient schemata to comprehend the passage?
- Can the child draw implications from the text?

## Syntax

The evaluation of syntax can be accomplished via written language sample analysis or by commercial measures like the Test of Syntactic Abilities (TSA) developed by Quigley, Steinkamp, Power, and Jones (1978). Cloze procedure is another effective method of assessing syntax. Moores (1978) indicates that cloze procedure provides more accurate information concerning syntax for children with language-based problems than do standardized instruments presently available.

It is important for evaluators and teachers to determine whether readers are limited to the mastery of base structure or whether they are able to determine meaning from passages that utilize complex structures and transformation. It should be remembered that short sentences are not necessarily easier sentences to comprehend. For example, the sentence, *The boy was hit,* is a complex passive deletion sentence that offers very little context. Passive sentences in themselves are difficult to comprehend. This example offers further challenge because the instrument (what hit the boy) is deleted. Therefore although the sentence contains only four words, it could present problems to young children or children with limited language abilities.

Russell, Power, and Quigley (1976) caution that many sentences used in the early level reading series are actually more difficult than those that appear in high school texts or common newstand material. Longer sentences may provide more context because they provide more information. Information-rich sentences can remain in base structure or at simple transformational levels; for example, *The first player accidentally hit the boy because he was standing too close to home plate.* However, if the information is presented in the form of a relative clause or other embedded form, a complex sentence also emerges; for example, *The boy that hit the girl that cried lives next door to that store.*

In evaluating syntax as related to reading, close attention must be given, therefore, to both the test material and the child. Although meaning is carried by syntax, the syntax itself can unnecessarily hinder comprehension of that meaning.

Questions the evaluator and/or teacher might address are:

- What kinds of sentences does the child use and understand in spoken language (e.g., simple base structure sentences, highly descriptive forms, series of short sentences linked by "and," question forms, negative transformations, relative and subordinate clauses, etc.)?
- Does the child use a variety of sentence structures in expressive writing?
- What are these structures?
- Does the child understand a variety of sentence structures in reading?
- What are these structures?

## Graphomorphophonemics

Graphomorphophonemic (GMP) concerns in evaluation have probably been overvalued and given a level of importance in assessment that is not deserved. If as much attention were given to the other psycho-sociolinguistic components, we would probably accomplish much more efficient and realistic evaluation and subsequent instruction.

There is little value in assessing single phonological elements (initial, medial, or final sounds) because they are not linguistically meaningful and have no pscyhological reality. In this connection, the following questions are suggested as guides in testing reading:

- Can the child syllabically recode a word?
- Does the child recognize and decode morphological elements?
- Does the child understand the linguistic purposes of punctuation, capitalization, spacing, and so on?

### Application of Diagnostic Reading Tests to the Model

As we have noted previously, we are reluctant to endorse the use of standardized reading tests for the evaluation of current functioning in reading because such measures tend to focus on the phonic and word-meaning aspects of the process with little attention to the other more influential psycho-socio-linguistic components. However, the teacher or evaluator can select portions of these available measures to test certain aspects of reading abilities. Caution must be exercised when selecting these subtests; it is important that the function of the selected subtest be based on the model rather than on what may be proposed in the test itself.

Table 5–1 summarizes diagnostic reading tests that have subtests from which specific information relating to the psycho-socio-linguistic model can be gained. As the table shows, many tests yield information for the recognition of consonants, vowels, letters, syllabic knowledge, and word recognition without context—all of which are GMP components. Additional GMP information on blends, rhyming, nonsense words, rate, and spelling can also be readily gained from these measures.

The only available test of syntactic abilities related to reading is the Test of Syntactic Abilities or TSA (Quigley, Steinkamp, Power, & Jones, 1978). However, this measure was not designed specifically for reading. It was developed to assess the syntactic abilities of hearing-impaired students, though it is currently being piloted for use with other populations. It is thus necessary for teachers or evaluators to rely primarily on their own knowledge of syntax and how it relates to the reading process in order to evaluate both the complexity of materials read and the student's use of syntax.

Table 5–1 also cites available standardized measures for evaluating some aspects of semantics. These aspects concern primarily word recognition in context, word opposites, and word definitions at the word level. Comprehension of phrases, sentences, and passages, both orally and silently read, can also be evaluated using these measures.

We are not aware of any standardized measures to evaluate either pragmatic or text-cohesion aspects of reading. Teachers and evaluators will need to depend on their own knowledge of these factors to analyze specific passages that demonstrate or violate rules in these components.

**Table 5-1  Application of the Model through Existing Diagnostic Reading Tests**

| GMP | Syntax | Semantics | Pragmatics | Test Cohesion |
|---|---|---|---|---|
| Consonant, vowel, letters, etc.:<br>Botel (1978)<br>Spache (1972)<br>Gates-McKillop (1962)<br>Roswell-Chall (1959)<br>Durrell (1955)<br>Stanford Diagnostic (1977)<br>Woodcock Reading Mastery (1973)<br><br>Blends:<br>Spache (1972)<br><br>Syllabication:<br>Botel (1978)<br>Spache (1972)<br>Gates-McKillop (1962)<br>Roswell-Chall (1959)<br>Silent Reading Test (1970)<br><br>Rhyming words:<br>Botel (1978)<br><br>Nonsense words:<br>Botel (1978)<br>Gates-McKillop (1962)<br><br>Spelling:<br>Durrell (1955)<br>Gates-McKillop (1962)<br><br>Word recognition (out of context):<br>Botel (1978)<br>Spache (1972)<br>Gates-McKillop (1962)<br>Silent Reading Test (1970)<br>Sipay (1974)<br>Stanford Diagnostic (1977)<br>Woodcock Reading Mastery (1973) | Test of Syntactic Abilities (1978) | Word recognition (in context):<br>Silent Reading Test (1970)<br>Stanford Diagnostic (1977)<br><br>Word opposites:<br>Botel (1978)<br><br>Word definitions:<br>Gates-McKillop (1962)<br>Nelson-Denny (1973)<br>Stanford Diagnostic (1977)<br><br>Phrase meaning:<br>Gates-McKillop (1962)<br>Woodcock Reading Mastery (1973)<br><br>Sentence comprehension:<br>Stanford Diagnostic (1977)<br><br>Passage comprehension:<br>Spache (1972)<br>Durrell (1955)<br>Gilmore (1968)<br>Nelson-Denny (1973)<br>Stanford Diagnostic (1977)<br>Woodcock Reading Mastery (1973) | | |

## SUMMARY

We suggest that teachers and evaluators take the time to understand the necessary foundations of language and its psycho-sociolinguistic components in order to apply such knowledge effectively and efficiently to the evaluation of reading. For too long, because of limitations in linguistic knowledge, we have concentrated on peripheral or low-level evaluation objectives and have been unable to approach comprehension successfully. Today, fortunately, such linguistic knowledge is becoming increasingly available.

# Chapter 6

# Reading Instruction

*A* *beautiful princess found him and gave him a magic kiss. . . .*

The focus of this chapter is on reading instruction and the implications of the model for the teaching of reading. Each of the psycho-socio-linguistic processes presented in Chapter 3 is elaborated with strategies to assist readers in hypothesis-testing in the respective psycho-socio-linguistic areas.

Jenkins et al. (1981) suggest that reading problems, specifically those related to comprehension, may be described more appropriately as language problems. The problems in comprehension have been described by Jenkins and Pany (1980) as deficits related to world knowledge, linguistic-reasoning ability, and attentional capabilities. If we are to address reading instruction that allows children mastery of written language, we must base our approach on a linguistic viewpoint, with attention directed toward those possible constraints that limit success in learning to read. As professionals charged with the responsibility of teaching reading, we must examine how we conduct that teaching. It is vital that the same reorientation and reconstruction needed in the formulation of a definition or the establishment of criteria for evaluation be applied to the methodology for reading instruction.

## THE BEGINNINGS OF READING

When has a child actually learned to read? Does reading mastery constitute the ability to pronounce correctly all of the words on a selected word list or to answer correctly all of the questions on a reading test in order to determine if the child is "at grade level?" Can reading instruction assume control of spoken language?

Before the issue of mastery can be addressed, we should first examine what occurs in the development of a child that will result in an ability to read. Professionals who hold a view of reading based on a process of developmental levels tend to posit stages through which children pass as they successfully facilitate reading accomplishment (Bush & Huebner, 1970; Harris, 1970; Kaluger & Kolson, 1969). Most of these explanations of the development of reading begin with a prereading stage. In general, the prereading stage is the time before the child is able to interpret visual representations of language. The corresponding age is assumed naturally to be during the preschool years. However, many children begin reading before formal school entry. Others do not master the process even by the end of the primary grades.

Although the imposing of stages or stage descriptions on the development of reading represents an attempt to demarcate various accomplishments made by emerging readers, several dangers can arise from such an attempt. Professionals, in searching for organizational guidelines, become tied to the idea of stages or levels and begin to force children into them based on age, grade, or skill criteria. If prereading is equated with the stage that typifies preschool children, level expectations by school entry will be that children will move to a more advanced stage, such as beginning reading or Grade Level 1. In reality, a stage or level concept is inaccurate. Development in reading, as in other areas of growth, is a process or continuum rather than a series of discrete stages or even overlapping levels. Development is a simultaneous interaction of several systems or subsystems rather than a sequential unfolding of rigid stages in parallel areas of maturation.

A 7-year-old child who is not yet reading may be classified as functioning at a prereading stage or kindergarten level in the light of evaluation and instructional goals. However, it is much more appropriate to view such a child in relation to what the child knows and does not know about reading. Although the child has most likely mastered the metareading aspects of reading, unlike the 3- or 4-year-old who would also be viewed as being at prereading stage, this child has not realized the strategies that will permit the decoding of meaning and a comprehension of what is being read. In other words, the child has knowledge of what books are and knows that print represents meaning and that words are strung together in sentences, and so on, but does not know how to generate necessary hypotheses and make decisions regarding written language.

Much discussion has emerged over the efficacy of "teaching" reading to young children. Proponents insist that early exposure to the printed form will ensure reading success in the school setting. The debate, however, centers on how formal or structured this early exposure should be. Will the activity of reading regularly to a child from an early age eventually yield early reading mastery? Must reading be taught in ways similar to methods employed at Grade 1 level in school reading programs? Are other approaches more appropriate to the accomplishment of success by early readers? Is early reading even a desirable feat to have preschool children accomplish? There is still much discussion concerning these and other related questions. However, examination of how young children master reading seemingly without the intervention of a "teacher" may provide answers that might usefully apply to beginning readers at any age.

### Observing Reading in Preschool Children

There are various views concerning the feasibility of teaching reading to preschoolers. Although these views share a basic agreement that many preschool children are in fact capable of reading mastery, the emphases and techniques differ.

Emery (1975), in addressing parents, targets Age 4 as a starting place for reading instruction for most children. He feels that parents can successfully implement a reading program. Other authors make somewhat exaggerated claims, for example, that teaching a preschool child to read can be accomplished in a period of 60 days (Ledson, 1975) when in reality the process extends over a significantly longer period of time. Though cautious about recommending early reading, White (1975) maintains that the educational and linguistic developments that begin when a child is as young as 8 to 9 months of age may be the most crucial. However, he cautions that commercially available reading kits that claim to aid in early reading preparation are basically attempts at "exploitation of the insecurities of American families" (p. 146).

In observing early readers, Torrey (1969) and Mather (1972) ask whether we really "teach" young children to read. Mather explains that most early readers accomplish the task at home rather than in an educational setting. She also notes that most early readers are read to by parents or by other adults and older children. Young readers are also unsophisticated in their knowledge of the alphabet or in the specifics of sound-symbol transfer. In other words, "cat" is cat, but grapheme-phoneme analysis is not consciously applied.

We maintain that "teaching" reading is something that may be done once children enter school. Such teaching constitutes the actual instruction of children in the use of the decoding strategies of the various psycho-socio-linguistic components, not the methdology traditionally considered to constitute reading instruction. Formalized strategies are not recommended for preschool children. The objectives that best serve children during the preschool years are those that emphasize experience and exposure to foster metareading knowledge. With very young children, before formal educational placement, the goal is not actually to instruct, but to facilitate the ability to read. If young children begin to interpret written language, they have then deduced how to use the strategies themselves and are therefore "ready" to accomplish the feat. Until this stage is reached, parents and preschool teachers should continue to foster an environment that will stimulate and motivate learning about reading that is a prerequisite to actual reading activity. In this way, the child is better prepared to receive instruction upon entry in the school and academic setting.

Söderbergh (1977), in recording the development of reading in her own preschooler, takes a more scholarly approach than some other authors. She describes in a case study how her child learned to read. There is no "hard sell" approach in her report, but the information has wide relevance. In addition, Söderbergh's study has value from both a linguistic and research standpoint. As Lado points out in the introduction to Söderbergh's publication, this is the "first full linguistic study of a case of reading acquisition . . . and interprets the data as part of acquiring a linguistic code" (p. xiv). Söderbergh applies an experimental linguistic method to her study of early reading. Lado explains that this involves "control of input under experimental conditions to test whether or not the child will acquire the code through experience in reading without specific formal teaching of the code itself . . . [as when] the child acquires [spoken] language" (p. xiv).

Here some questions arise: If a child learns to speak in a native tongue without formal teaching but through language exposure in social context, is it not reasonable to assume that the same process should evolve with respect to the written aspect of language? Is it possible that exposure to written language at an early age allows the child to investigate, to form hypotheses and to discover the code of written language? Why is it that some children learn to read by what appears to be mere observation of text while having stories read to them?

Söderbergh postulates that if a child learns to read without formal teaching during the preschool years, while developing spoken language, the child acquires mastery of written form both through and in conjunction with speech. While hearing stories being read, the child discovers relationships between what is spoken and the printed representation. The child is able to unravel the code of written language and to integrate the relationships with a growing spoken code. Söderbergh emphasizes that this occurs not only in phoneme-grapheme relationships but in syntax and semantics as well. We would expand her hypothesis even further to include the psycho-sociolinguistic components of pragmatics and text cohesion or format.

In discussing her study of early reading, Söderbergh points up the problem of determining a way of exposing the young child to written language. She states that children accomplish spoken language through exposure to the speech of others that constantly surrounds them and through their own mutual communication. However, the nature of written language makes this natural exposure somewhat more difficult to attain. Söderbergh observes that the obvious examples of written language within a child's environment are seldom geared toward the child's interests or language level. Therefore, an effort must be made to allow such a presentation in other ways.

We would tend to disagree with Söderbergh's view concerning the availability of written language examples. Reading functions for us whether we are perusing cereal boxes or studying a dissertation on cochlear implants. What is important for the preschool child is the exposure to various *forms* of reading, since the goal is the internalization of what reading is about. As children develop speech, they are not first exposed to words, then phrases or sentences, and finally discourse. In the development of spoken language, children are surrounded by the richness of speech communication and all that spoken conversation entails. Thus, children learn what communication is about and can then successfully master the activity for themselves.

## Early Reading Directions in School

Observation of young children and the current level of knowledge related to child development should make it obvious that each child entering formal education at kindergarten or first grade possesses a different linguistic, social, emotional, physical, intellectual, and experiential history. However, in reality parents and many professionals still equate the turning of age 6 with the ability to read. As stated previously, some children begin reading at age 3, while others may not reach this linguistic level or even desire to learn to read until they are 8 or 9 years of age. This variation may be due to any number or combination of factors unique to the individual child. Such factors may either enhance or delay the child's facility for reading.

Farr (1972) emphasizes that beginning readers must develop an understanding and awareness that relationships exist among printed words. Meaning relations exist within the key structural elements, both in and between sentences. Reading instruction by a single-word approach or by presenting vocabulary solely in isolation of text fails to take into account the vital interactive effect of context passage meaning. For example, "house" represents a meaning different from "in the house." It is critical that the beginning reader be presented with vocabulary in such a way that meaning can be derived based on context. The early reader must develop the ability to grasp the interrelated meanings without particular attention to the reading of the words in isolation from one another.

The ability to relate printed information to experience is crucial to meaning. If there is no prior experience of the reality, either actual or vicarious, meaning does not occur. In this case, the written symbol has no basis for interpretation. K. Goodman (1969) explains that readers select enough from the available information to predict a language structure that they can decode. This applies not only to syntax but to the other decoding strategies as well. For this to occur, the reader must possess related prior experience as a meaning base. Reading material must be within the child's experiential repertoire. Weber (1970) concludes from her studies with first grade students that early readers expect sentences to conform to a language structure they already know and actively use. This further emphasizes the point that reading instruction and materials need to be within the current language capacity of the child.

### Reading and the Language Experience

Reading instruction that favors a language-experience approach suggests the value and need of experience in teaching reading at a theoretical level. In practice, however, such instruction falls short of the task because of oversimplification in the use of the content of experience as applied to reading. The experience of a field trip or class activity should accomplish more than a mere coding of an experience into a form that results in an experience chart. In many cases, an experience or event provides enough reading material for a book, but in fact it is drastically reduced to a short story or perhaps even a few short sentences. If a language experience approach is truly realized, the focus must move from generally reiterating the experience to fully reconstructing the experience in written language. This entails a move beyond the basic essay or description form to the use of a narrative representation of the occasion.

Ordinarily, the use of an experience might result in the following production:

> We went to the circus.
> We saw clowns.
> We saw elephants.
> We saw acrobats.
> We saw lions.
> We ate popcorn.
> We ate peanuts.
> We had fun.

This is a utilization of a field trip experience recorded in an essay format with an attempt to emphasize a particular syntactic pattern (N + V + O) and certain vocabulary words (we, saw, ate). Based on this type of exposure and input, can we really wonder why children produce stories or essays not in their true format but in the format of the experience chart.

The experience of going to the circus has a wealth of valuable and exciting information that deserves exploitation. The following essay format might be more stimulating and linguistically educational:

## A DAY AT THE CIRCUS

All of the children in Mrs. Smith's class helped plan the trip to the circus. Mrs. Smith called the bus company. Patty and Mary ordered the tickets.

On Monday, March 4, 1980, we brought our lunches to school. The bus drove away at 9:00 A.M. The ride took 1 hour and 25 minutes. Everyone sang songs on the bus.

The circus was in the Omni. We stood in line and gave the man our tickets. We sat four rows from the top of the building and could see everything.

The music started and the circus parade marched around. Everyone clapped and cheered. The ring master introduced the lion tamer and the lions. The lions jumped through rings of fire.

The next act was the Flying Rolondas. They walked on the high wire without a net. Everyone held their breath.

Finally the clowns came out. They did tricks and everyone laughed and clapped. They were the last circus act.

By 3:00 P.M. we were all tired and ready to go back to school. Jimmy threw up on the bus because he ate too much junk food. But we had a good time anyway.

This form of recording an experience is of course much longer than the usual experience chart. However, it could be developed over a period of days with each chapter focusing on one unique aspect of the circus experience. In this way, the children could reconstruct and share their collected data concerning the field trip.

Note that the sentences in the essay vary in syntactic pattern and length, based on the meaning to be conveyed rather than on predetermined sentence patterns or target vocabulary. The purpose of syntax is to convey meaning, not to restrict it. Therefore, the use of a variety of sentences at an appropriate linguistic level (primarily base structure and early trans- formations) is more appropriate than a series of boring, short, stilted sentences. Note too that the sentences selected (active declarative sen- tences) are peculiar to the essay format.

In addition to the use of syntax as a function of format, our example conveys considerable information about the text cohesion of an essay. The underlying intent of the writing is to record or provide information for some audience: parents, other classes, and so on.

The same experience can be recorded in other formats, such as in a newspaper report, a letter to another class, or a story. The writing of a story based on a trip to the circus might take the form of individual children dictating or writing substories on a particular aspect of the circus that they found most interesting. These stories might then be compiled into a larger story or book about the circus experience. For example, the following story about a clown might serve as one chapter or section in a class collection of individual writings.

## WHAT TO DO IF YOU HAVE A BIG RED NOSE

Once upon a time, there was a man who had a very big, round, red nose. Everybody laughed at him. This made him cry. Then his nose got redder and bigger.

One day he was sitting on his porch. A car with a loudspeaker drove by. A voice said, "Be a clown. Come to City Hall at 1:00 P.M. for tryouts." He thought this was a good idea. He could juggle anything, and he had a big red nose. So he went to the tryouts.

The man juggled apples and boxes and tomatoes and even eggs. Everybody cheered and clapped.

The circus boss loved the man's act and thought his nose was a wonderful clown nose. The man joined the circus and became the boss of all the clowns.

This child's story about becoming a clown is produced in story format, as described in Chapter 3. It contains a setting, a time reference, a hero with a dilemma, two episodes, and a resolution with a happy ending. While this example is somewhat longer than the original experience-chart presenta- tion, it is more like the stories found in books that children typically read at early grade levels.

Abrahamson (1980) has performed analyses of picture story books that children selected as their favorites. His findings were that children pre- ferred story books with "(1) episodic plots involving (2) confrontation with a problem and (3) characters who have opposing points of view or experience the same thing in contrasting ways'' (p. 169). He further found that 50 percent of the preferred books contained elements of fantasy.

## Summary

When children begin to read and meet in printed form the concepts, words, and meanings they have previously acquired via their experience and development of spoken language, they are able to relate or match these with the printed words they read. In order to read, children must have a basic competence in language, that is, the ability to use phonology, syntax, semantics, and pragmatics to relate a code to meaning.

## READING INSTRUCTION—APPLICATION OF THE MODEL

### An Alternative Approach

Despite the continuous debate between proponents of reading instruction based on developing skills to enhance the ability to recode to the auditory mode to decode meaning and those who advocate a comprehension point of view that emphasizes decoding via other strategies, the weighting is still toward recoding to the auditory and the skill end of the seesaw. This skewed orientation has been representative of educators charged with the task of reading instruction with both normal children and those with various handicaps that limit reading mastery. Jenkins et al. (1981) point out that, like reading instruction designed for the general population of students, reading intervention or remediation techniques are based on a philosophical view in support of recoding skills. They state that authors as well as educators hold that remediation instruction should be based on recoding to gain meaning, on the assumption that such recoding is "a prerequisite for comprehension" (p. 28). Based on certain research, (Becker, 1977; Guthrie & Tyler, 1977) support for a recoding or GMP emphasis may appear initially to be warranted.

On the other hand, Smith and Goodman (1971) and other comprehension proponents oppose a recoding or GMP emphasis in instruction because of the fragmentation of the linguistic code that recoding causes. Compared with research in support of recoding-based instruction, there is very little that favors an emphasis on comprehension through other strategies. The reason becomes obvious when one recognizes that recoding has been the central focus and ultimate key to comprehension for the past 50 years. Now, however, what is needed is a padlock combination rather than the recoding skeleton key to unlock the meaning of written language.

This longstanding debate has one common point of agreement—that an understanding of what is read is the end goal. The variation in procedure stems from the path or strategy employed to reach that goal. The final outcome remains the same: understanding the message communicated via the printed page. In the traditional definition of decoding, the level of entry to comprehension is at the GMP, or more specifically, recoding rung of the written conversation ladder (see Figure 3-1). We do not now suggest that such entry should be totally omitted but that it be placed in proper perspective in relation to the other linguistic components.

*Graphomorphophonemics*

Using the analogy of a ladder leading to a loft with the loft representing comprehension and the ladder the process of reading, one can view decoding of GMP information as the lowest rung. The goal, of course, is to gain a clear view of the loft above. The first rung, GMP, gives some view of the loft above, but in fact it is the least helpful in determining or attaining the end goal of understanding. With an instruction methodology that emphasizes only the decoding of meaning at this level, we provide the child with a strategy that makes the viewing of comprehension extremely difficult.

*Syntax*

The second rung of the ladder represents syntax. At this level of decoding, aspects of the sentence are highlighted as important or subordinate. For example, in the sentence *The girl who lives next door is my friend*, the information that *the girl is my friend* is deemed more important than the fact that she *lives next door*. The priority information is cued by its position as a main clause. The subordinate information, which serves to describe the girl, is cued through the syntactic form of a relative clause. Syntactic forms thus allow a somewhat improved yet still shadowed view of the comprehension loft; the reader is still not using the most effective way of observing meaning. Knowledge of the rules of syntax, governed by word position and sentence transformation, aids in ultimate comprehension but is not the most effective and efficient level of entry (Franks & Bransford, 1974). If we emphasize instruction only at the syntactic level, we limit the child to a guessing game bound by sentence patterns.

*Semantics*

Decoding also occurs through lexical selection, which is semantics or meaning operating at the word level. Many methodologies equate this narrow interpretation of meaning with derivation of the larger or central meaning of the text. Reading instruction, however, must expand beyond the single word or "whole word" approach. Definitions of a word without the nuances and modifications of the other words of the phrase, sentence, or passage preclude awareness of the true meaning of the word in the given context. Y. Goodman (1970) underscores this by explaining that words should never be introduced out of the context of language because it is the context that alters the grammatical function of words and their syntactic relationships with other words. Context will also provide clues to specific and appropriate meaning, pronunciation and intonation pattern.

## Pragmatics

Decoding information at the pragmatic level, or the viewing of comprehension from the fourth rung, permits an even clearer view. Pragmatic cues in written language allow for the necessary understanding of old and new information through the presence of determiners, pronominalization, and other referent forms. For example, in the sentence *She went to see her friend*, *she* and *her* represent a person already made apparent in earlier sentences. However, in a careful examination of early readers, such sentences can be seen to occur without any previous indication of who *she* or *it* or *that* might be. In the above case, *she* may have been used because it was a selected vocabulary word in a reading lesson, while its true value in terms of a pragmatic function was violated or ignored.

Pragmatics also facilitates a view of comprehension through sentence cohesion. In written conversation, the author must relate the sentences to allow presentation of meaning. The first sentence relates to the second sentence and so on, each sentence elaborating and providing additional clues to the intent of the writer. The comprehension loft is now being viewed from a more effective point of observation.

## Text Cohesion

The fifth rung in the reading process ladder is text cohesion. Reading instruction should stress decoding at this level for clues as to whether the written format is a story, letter, essay, and so on. Decoding at this level allows the reader to determine parameters as to what the written conversation is all about. It permits a determination of the setting and orientation or stage the writer wishes to set in the communication effort.

## Semantics Expanded

The top rung of the ladder, which allows the clearest view of comprehension, is semantics. Semantics, as we have noted, is not just the word meaning of individual vocabulary words. It also involves meaning that results from word relationships. To present a student with a vocabulary word such as *house* with an accompanying definition specific to that entity does not guarantee the student will understand the concept expressed in the relationship of the words *in the house* or in the sentence *The children are in the house*. Semantics in the ultimate sense is the comprehension of the holistic meaning of the written conversation. This is accomplished through the mutual and simultaneous interactive clues that each of the process components provides. The successful reader at the top rung has used all of the ladder levels together to reach the comprehension loft.

The implication of this analogy is that children must be taught from a much broader perspective than just decoding, a relatively ineffective entry point to comprehension. Written language operates through the interaction of all the components, not just the one as we have forced children to select in traditional reading instruction. A successful reader, in conversation with an author, uses multiple strategic clues to determine what is being communicated. Therefore, it is vital that the multiple strategies be part of reading instruction. Perhaps this point was stated most succinctly by Hickman (1977): To the question, "What do fluent readers do?" she answers quite simply, "They read" (p. 375).

**Looking Down from the Loft**

Theories of reading differ in their assumptions about the locus of meaning. One theory states that meaning is contained within the text, and it is the reader's task to uncover or decode that meaning (Carroll & Chall, 1975; Chall, 1967; Gibson & Levin, 1975). An alternative theory states that the reader brings meaning to the text, thereby confirming or disconfirming the reader's hypotheses or expectations (K. Goodman, 1967; F. Smith, 1975). Many programs have been directed toward developing subskills of letter recognition, word recognition, and sound blending to decode meaning.

Olson (1977) proposes that the issues of language structure, comprehension, logical reasoning, and learning to speak and read can be traced to underlying assumptions about whether meaning is or is not contained within the sentence. The type of instructional program selected would, of course, follow from the selected assumptions. F. Smith (1977) suggests that two insights are requisites to learning to read: (1) print is meaningful and (2) written language and speech differ. While these requisites may appear simplistic, they are infrequently researched and frequently ignored in instruction.

To continue our analogy of the ladder to the loft, the person who brings meaning to the task of reading has the vantage point of sitting in the loft peering down. This reader brings meaning to the text as a result of past experiences, previous learning, and knowledge of the schema of the text itself. At this point of entry to the reading activity, assumptions or hypotheses can be made with a full view of the intended message of the author. Since the reader is already in the loft, the largest scope of reference is available because the greatest amount of context is at hand. The more context in evidence, the easier it is to attain comprehension. The reader in the loft can peer down, viewing all of the strategy levels and determine which will be needed to verify or confirm meaning.

## STRATEGIES FOR READING INSTRUCTION

This section is not intended to be a curriculum guide; there are numerous guides, cookbooks, and recipes for reading instruction available elsewhere. The intent is rather to present some ideas for instruction in each of the areas described in the model. Hopefully, these will in turn set the idea generator of the reader/teacher into motion to develop more ideas and produce additional guidelines for the reader/teacher to use in sifting through the available ideas and in selecting appropriate strategies for instruction. Instruction in only one area (text, pragmatic, semantic, syntactic, graphomorphophonemic) can be a disservice to the child who needs to learn to use all the systems simultaneously. Yet most available reading programs still teach isolated skills out of meaningful context.

Some programs in critical thinking address the issue of logical inference in reading texts (Lowerre & Scandura, 1973–1974) beginning at a fairly early level, such as second grade. In our opinion, this type of reading is preferred to many of the mundane tales in the typical basal reader series. Some programs that claim to be total communication/arts programs are in fact concerned with experiences that reflect both knowledge and use of language (Botel & Seaver, 1980). However, such programs might be directed only to responses to literature, selection of reading materials, written and oral composition, or semantic analysis of language patterns for more advanced readers rather than to an emphasis on early phases of reading acquisition.

### Storytelling

Storytelling as a focus for reading instruction has been examined by Broman (1975) and Stewig (1978). They describe the advantages of storytelling and offer some guidelines for storytelling time. Their suggestions for teachers include reading the story aloud several times for practice before reading to the children, recording the story, analyzing the recordings, devising an introduction to the story, practicing the story in front of a mirror, and adding facial and bodily expression as needed. In other words, storytelling should not be an "off-the-top-of-one's-head" activity, but rather a competency to be rehearsed and developed.

As Stewig (1978) notes, storytelling in schools is lacking. This may be due to the demands on the time of teachers. Storytelling competence requires time and practice to develop. We agree with Stewig that the development of competency in storytelling is well worth the time spent. In our view, storytelling is a prime requisite in the development of underlying reading knowledge. In addition to assisting the mastery of reading in the child, storytelling provides an opportunity for the teacher to share and experience some of the rich traditions of literature that may be beyond the current reading levels of the students. Amato, Emans, and Ziegler (1973) found storytelling to be effective also in developing self-image, empathy, and creativity in children.

Sutton-Smith (1975) has emphasized the importance of having the children do the storytelling. He reports that, if teachers repeatedly request stories from children and demonstrate interest in them, more and better stories will emerge. Continued development in narrative competence will also occur and ultimately lead to a desire on the part of the students to write as well as tell stories. Sutton-Smith considers storytelling narrative to be an art form. He suggests that the reason so little of it has been done in schools is that the arts have never been considered a major component of the curriculum.

In initiating storytelling by children, it may be necessary to build rapport with them, since all children are not willing to engage in the activity. Sutton-Smith found that children who were reluctant or refused to tell stories were those whose relationships with their parents, teachers, or other children were uncomfortable or disrupted in some way. The children who were eager to tell stories and were high fantasizers had parents who had told them many imaginative stories from early ages on.

Sutton-Smith also found that a remarkable proportion of children's stories include some aspect of conflict and that children between the ages of 5 and 10 progress through several levels in telling stories or in the development of narrative competence. Based on Maranda and Maranda's (1971) classifications of stories or tales with conflict, Sutton-Smith (1975) presents four levels of responses:

> *Level I.* The most common response at this level is that the subject is threatened or overcome by a monster or there is a lack or deprivation to which no response is made. In a few cases, we are only told of the presence of the monster with some implied threat, or someone else is hurt, or we are scared, or the monster

is described. One thinks of paralysis in the face of fear when seeking the biological counterparts to this response . . .

*Level II*. The predominant responses here are those of escaping or being rescued. The monster may be attacked but the attack is not successful. This is what the Marandas term "failed mediation." In this subject group, some children convert the monster into a benevolent creature. One may join with him in attacking others, or simply make him a nondangerous entity. On occasion, the benevolent monster has to persuade the mother (now the negative force) that he may be taken into the home quite safely. Unlike most fairy tales and folktales, there is little reference amongst this group to the interference of magic or luck, an indication perhaps of the inner rather than the outer directedness of this particular population. In most cases, those who rescue us do not succeed in getting rid of the original threat either, so that these are level II responses . . .

*Level III*. At this level, the story's central character is successful in rendering the threat powerless in some ways or in overcoming what is lacking. The enemy may withdraw. The nullification of the threat may be done by the good services of others . . .

*Level IV*. At this level the danger is not only removed, there is a complete transformation, so that there is clearly no possibility of this threat or this lack returning again. (pp. 88–89)

The findings based on Sutton-Smith's research were that the plot in stories developed with age, girls developed more than boys after age 6, boys told stories with a powerful figure overcoming a weaker one more often than girls, girls often resolved conflict by alliances between a second power and a weaker power, and boys most frequently told stories of villainy while girls told stories of a lack or deprivation. It would thus appear that the cultural differences of growing up as a boy or girl are reflected in the process of telling stories. The authors of the Right to Read Project at the Florida School for the Deaf and Blind have described some approaches to stoytelling for use with hearing-impaired children (Shetler & Simon, 1980). These approaches could be applied to other groups as well.

### Storyreading

Storyreading can be done by parents, but it is also an important part of the instructional program in the classroom, since it does not always occur before young children enter school. Storyreading can be used as a basic strategy by the teacher to help facilitate the development of all the systems we have described as necessary for the acquistion of reading appreciation and competence.

An environment similar to that used in reading at home is advised. Instead of the teacher or aide standing in front of the class reading a story to all of the children, it is more effective to read stories to smaller groups of children in places more suited to the activity, such as the floor, in rocking chairs, or in other more comfortable environments, so that the idea of reading for pleasure, which implies being comfortable during the process, can be achieved.

We have had experiences in teaching our own children to read or, more appropriately, in "viewing" our own children and other preschoolers engage in hypothesis-testing behavior leading to reading. The process begins with reading frequently to the child. More and more books become part of the household library. The child spends a fair amount of time interacting with the books, exploring them, patting them, flipping the pages. The child frequently looks at the person reading the book, then interacts more directly with the book by looking at it for long periods (perhaps a minute or more). The child then becomes more active. A reading position, as described by McDermott (1977), may be assumed, for example, by climbing into a favorite chair or by lying on the floor. The child may begin pointing to a section on the page that matches what is being told by the reader. The child then gradually tells the story (in later instances verbatim) and predicts what comes next. The child may know there is a story to be uncovered. In some cases, this knowledge, as with hearing-impaired children, may appear to be more advanced than the indicated linguistic production levels. The hearing child can usually retell favorite stories, stating goals and resolutions.

Obviously, a significant contribution to context and comprehension is provided by nonlinguistic cues, such as pictures, as well as by linguistic ones. Both of these types of cues are related to the text (e.g., knowledge from the physical format of the book, where it begins and ends, where the title page is) as well as to the context of reading (e.g., how people sit or recline when they read, i.e., the position assumed). Thus, it is evident that text cohesion can involve the general format of written language (Is it a letter, a note, a story, a sign?) at the primitive levels of reading and can also become a very complex aspect of sentence-to-sentence relationships at a more advanced level.

## Text Cohesion

The text of written material provides many formalized cues to aid the reader in acquiring the meaning intended by the other party in the conversation, namely the author. Obvious cues to text can be included in the discussion that usually accompanies the reading. For example: consider the following exchange over a personal letter from Sally (Exhibit 6-1).

> J:  Yea! We got a letter from Sally.
> S:  When did she send it?
> J:  On Tuesday.
> S:  Ooh, it took 5 days to get here.
> J:  Let's see what's new with Sally.
> S:  Open it! Open it!

What possible hypotheses could be formed from the above interaction? The following are possibilities:

$H_1$   A date or other heading may be present.

$H_2$   The letter will begin with a greeting: "Dear _____."

$H_3$   A polite written conversational form will follow: "Hope you both are well."

$H_4$   The paragraph form will carry information concerning the author.

$H_5$   A question format will carry a request of information from the reader.

---

**Exhibit 6-1**  The Personal Letter

---

June 1, 1981—Monday

Dear Joan and Suzanne,
   Hope you both are well. We are all OK out here in the far West.
   I went hiking last week and it was a real thrill. I have never witnessed such awesome beauty before in my entire life. I also met a rather captivating guide who was *very* helpful in explaining how to tie my hiking boots. Need I say more?
   What is happening in summer school? Joan, are you still feuding with old Professor J. about your paper? Suzanne, have you heard from your friend in Denver?
   Well that's all for now!

Love and kisses,

Sally

P.S. Send money—I'm broke.

---

$H_6$   A polite termination of conversation will occur: "That's all for now."

$H_7$   The formal closing will be written: "Love and kisses."

$H_8$   The signature will stand alone: "Sally."

$H_9$   A postscript may be added (but not required): "P.S. Send money."

The format of written language, in addition to confirming or refuting existing hypotheses, suggests new hypotheses. For example, the beginning, "Once a very long time ago in a faraway land. . . ," serves to generate a hypothesis of an upcoming tale, somewhat mythical and romantic in kind, whereas a sentence like, "Just because John thinks he will get what he wants. . . ," indicates a more direct, less inferential, statement of affairs that probably has nothing to do with the castle in the first text.

Text cohesion can also be viewed from a perspective of how sentences relate to each other. The first sentence usually offers a topic that is elucidated by subsequent sentences. Consider the following example.

> John took on the responsibilities of the chairmanship eagerly during the middle of the summer. By November, the picture had become quite bleak. Without the complete support system and the moments of inspiration to which he had grown accustomed, he was unable to fulfill his dream of fame, power, and conquest and began to look once more for the tranquility that had always eluded him.

Here, the first sentence introduces the topic in terms of the main character (the experiencer), his position, and his general emotional frame of mind. The second sentence presents a time reference and describes an emotional change in the experiencer, who is now assumed rather than specifically mentioned. The third sentence alludes to the reasons for the change in the experiencer's emotional state, and the experiencer is referenced through pronominalization.

From this example, it may be seen that text is much more than a string of casually connected sentences. Each sentence has cohesion or a tie with all preceding sentences (anaphoric reference). Some sentences also have ties with sentences that follow (cataphoric reference) (Halliday & Hasan, 1976).

Many early reading books, as parts of a basal series, fail to utilize this aspect of text cohesion. The following examples illustrate this point.

Cowboy Red

Red was a cowboy.
He was a big man.
Red could ride a horse.
He could catch a cow.

(From *Sidewalks* by W. J. Iverson and F. W. Dehansey, New York: L. W. Singer Co., 1969, p. 33. Reprinted by permission.)

By rewriting stories like this, a type that commonly appears in early level readers, the advantages of text cohesion in the decoding process can be observed and used by the child in reading. For example:

Cowboy Red

Red was a cowboy.
He was a big man.
He could ride a horse and catch a cow.

By making the sentences longer but not necessarily more complex, this simple rewrite helps supply the context of text cohesion that is vital to comprehension.

At an expanded level, the story in Figure 6–1 could be rewritten to portray more clearly the story's meaning by supplying text cohesion. This story, as in most early reading level texts, contains pictures that provide the initial contact with context.

In reading, it would seem logical that text and picture support one another. Such is not the case in the Figure 6–1 example. The story, which is informative or essay in format, has a message, which is that Carlos does not speak English and is therefore limited in social interaction because of his language barrier. The pictures and text should cooperatively present this information. In this example, however, not only do the contexts not cooperate, they are inappropriate. The first picture in no way relates to Carlos's problem, except that he is indeed alone.

The first violation of text cohesion is in the title. This is not an essay about a watch, but one about a boy who cannot speak the same language as the other children in school. A better title might be: Why is Carlos Sad? or Why is Carlos Lonely?

McConnell (1979) stresses the importance of the title, not only in telling what a passage is about, but also "how the story [or passage] feels about what it is about" (p. 27). The text of the Figure 6–1 story fails to fulfill the

**Figure 6–1** The Story of the Watch

*Carlos got a watch.*
*TICK-TICK-TICK went the watch.*
*Carlos said not one word.*

*"Let me see the watch," said Bud.*
*TICK-TICK-TICK went the watch.*
*Carlos said not one word.*

*"Carlos got a watch!" said Bud.*
*"Can I see it, too?" said Bill.*
*TICK-TICK-TICK went the watch.*
*Carlos said not one word.*

*Many boys came.*
*They came to look at the watch.*

*TICK-TICK-TICK went the watch.*
*Carlos said not one word.*

*TICK-TICK-TICK went the watch.*
*All of the boys went to play,*
*for Carlos said not one word.*

Source: *I Aim, Ask and Act. Don't Tell* by J. M. Franco, J. M. Kelley, and T. Whitman, New York: American Book Company, 1970, p. 32. Reprinted by permission of D.C. Heath and Co.

**Figure 6-1** continued

Carlos got a watch.
TICK-TICK-TICK went the watch.
Carlos said not one word.

**Figure 6–1** continued

''Let me see the watch,'' said Bud.
TICK-TICK-TICK went the watch.
Carlos said not one word.

**Figure 6–1** continued

"Carlos got a watch," said Bud.
"Can I see it, too?" said Bill.
TICK-TICK-TICK went the watch.
Carlos said not one word.

**Figure 6–1** continued

Many boys came.
They came to look at the watch.
TICK-TICK-TICK went the watch.
Carlos said not one word.

**Figure 6–1** continued

TICK-TICK-TICK went the watch.
All of the boys went to play,
for Carlos said not one word.

purpose of the essay format, which is to present (not withhold) direct and specific information to the reader. A rewrite might take the following form:

Carlos is all alone on the playground.
He has no one to play with.
He has a new watch and he is listening to it.

Bud walks up to Carlos.
He listens to the watch.
Bud talks to Carlos, but he does not talk to Bud.
Carlos cannot speak English.

Bill walks up to Carlos and Bud.
He listens to the watch.
Bud and Bill talk to Carlos, but he does not talk to them.

Some more boys walk up.
They all listen to the watch and talk to Carlos, but he talks to no one.

All of the boys except Carlos go to play a game.
He is all alone again.
He cannot speak English and he cannot understand what the boys tell him.
That is why Carlos is sad and lonely.

Though stories or essays that appear in reading series have very sophisticated messages that children are expected to gain from the text, the severe limitations imposed by a controlled vocabulary and/or syntax patterns make the comprehension of the target idea outrageously difficult.

To facilitate use of text cohesion at a simple level of instruction, cues in reading can serve as a simulation of storytelling or storyreading procedures in which the teacher points out these aspects of the text. Children who are read to frequently deduce these aspects themselves. At a more complex level, it may be necessary to direct instruction specifically toward looking for those entities that tie Sentence 1 to Sentence 2 to Sentence 3.

The simple level can be facilitated by exposure to various kinds of formats (notes, letters, essays, story types, etc.) to help the child predict or hypothesize the kind of form about to be read. It is obviously incumbent upon the teacher to become familiar with the various formats in children's books, which are generally either essay or story format, and with the way the format relates to the function of the written language. The functions might be to describe animals and their habitats, to relate a fairy tale, or to tell an animal narrative. The teacher's goal should be to provide a rich experiential interaction with a variety of books, stories, and other written language forms.

## Pragmatic

Pragmatic strategies for instruction can be closely interwoven with those that encourage text cohesion. How the paragraphs of a text present a topic and relate to each other is a context for pragmatic analysis and instruction. In addition, each sentence carries an underlying intent that in itself is also context. Major pragmatic interests have to do with the encoding of old and new information (Clark & Haviland, 1974) and the tying together of paragraphs. The noun at the beginning of the text introduces new information. Pronominalization signifies that the information is now old information. Tense holds the paragraph together by signaling that the focus remains on old information. While tense markers serve this purpose in written language, it is usually conveyed through intonational patterns in spoken language.

Returning to the example of a personal letter (Exhibit 6–1), let us consider the possible pragmatic hypotheses:

$H_1$ The salutation is analogous to the greeting in spoken language. It opens the conversation.

$H_{1a}$ The readers are presumed to be in the same vicinity.

$H_2$ The first two sentences imply turntaking.

$H_3$ The intent of Paragraph 2 is to present and discuss new information.

$H_{3a}$ Sentence 1 presents new information.

$H_{3b}$ Sentence 1 uses pronominalization to allude to old information ("it" = old information and refers back to "hiking," which was presented earlier in the sentence).

$H_{3c}$ Sentence 3 uses relativization to allude to old information ("who" = old information and refers back to "guide," which was presented earlier in the sentence).

$H_{3d}$ Sentence 4 refers to previously shared information by author and reader. The readers must infer or presuppose meaning based on previous experience with the author.

$H_4$ The underlying intent of Paragraph 3 is to request a response or return letter.

$H_5$ The conversation is terminated.

In this letter, presuppositions concerning the reading level were made on the part of the author, which determined the specific selection of linguistic complexity.

In Figure 6–1, the passage in a basal reader, we observe that the possibility of making pragmatic hypotheses is greatly frustrated and impeded. However, the rewrite allows the formulation of hypotheses at a pragmatic level. In the rewrite:

$H_1$   The underlying intent of the passage is to tell something.

$H_2$   New information is coded in the first sentence by the presentation of the topic (Carlos) and the problem (he is alone).

$H_3$   Old information is cued through pronominalization and consistency of tense.

$H_4$   Presupposition assumes awareness that language is used in social interaction and that without it a child is socially isolated.

$H_5$   The consistency of the essay ties the sentences and paragraphs together.

Pragmatic strategies must help readers uncover the restrictions placed by the first sentence on the succeeding sentences. A sentence-by-sentence processing strategy, which is frequently apparent in language/reading programs and experience charts, can mislead readers and deprive them of necessary strategies for decoding the meaning that was planned by the authors through such elegant writing techniques as implicature, which was used in the story of John assuming the responsibilities of a chairmanship.

**Semantic**

It is difficult to separate semantic strategies from those on other rungs of the ladder, since interdependence is the key to the entire process. Obviously, the acquisition of a larger vocabulary should facilitate more specific meaning, but unfortunately vocabulary acquisition alone does not aid greatly in the reading process. Once the basic schema has been mastered, however, a well-endowed lexicon is most helpful in the advanced levels of reading.

Semantic hypotheses can be formulated concerning the Exhibit 6–1 letter to Joan and Suzanne from Sally. For example:

$H_1$   The month, date, year, and day of the week indicate the time the letter was composed.

$H_2$    All vocabulary was selected by the author to be comprehensible by her readers.

$H_3$    Paragraph 1 implies concern for her close friends and assures them of her own well-being.

$H_4$    Paragraph 2 relates an episode. The resolution, however, is left to the reader.

$H_5$    Paragraph 3 implies underlying concern for her friends and the desire for return communication.

$H_6$    The termination of the letter indicates the author has finished the conversation.

$H_7$    The polite closing assures her friends of their affectionate bond.

$H_8$    The postscript implies that the author's funds are fast dwindling; and, if the readers take the statement seriously, they should indeed oblige. However, the meaning is really open-ended, so they will most likely take it as a bit of humor.

Unlike the case of the Exhibit 6–1 letter, semantic hypotheses are limited beyond the single word level in the basal reader story of Figure 6–1 (watch, came, Carlos, etc.) However, in the rewrite, the vocabulary words are not only presented several times but are presented in elaborate context, thereby allowing the child to discern meaning more easily. In addition, the entire meaning underlying the passage is not inferred; it is specifically stated, thereby fulfilling the purpose of the essay format.

Strategies for determining the semantic structure underlying the reading material can be facilitated by the teacher. At an early level, simple exposure to a wide array of written forms of stories and other kinds of formats should assist the reader in deducing the underlying schema. The selection of specific kinds of stories, for example, should facilitate hypothesis-testing skills in those categories of stories. For example, stories with a scene-setting, a hero who enters early in the story and assists in character and plot development, a goal not too unlike goals within the reader's own experience, and a series of episodes leading to a resolution of the major goal can be read, reconstructed, and even rewritten by the child.

Instead of the usual inane comprehension-testing questions like, What color was the boy's shirt? which has nothing to do with any of the major aspects of the story, some questions should be directed to those pertinent aspects of the story to assist in aiding recall. Such questions might include, Where does the story action take place? Who is the hero? What problem must the hero solve? Questions following the reading should focus on major aspects of the story structure rather than on inconsequential, descriptive information. It also would be helpful to ask the children if particular sentences in a passage are important (e.g. the goal sentence as opposed to a color description of a meadow). This would assist their search for significant and summary statements in the text.

Assistance to students in learning how to decipher the gist of passages is just as important as efforts directed toward understanding the semantic structure. The development of vocabulary or semantic word-level acquisition has received some attention in reading instruction. In her discussion ("Why We Burned our Basic Sight Vocabulary Cards") of reading instruction in which word lists or sight vocabulary cards are used, Hood (1974) emphasizes that such an approach denies the contextual meaning of words. She supports K. Goodman (1973) in stressing that words should not be taught in isolation apart from the context of phrase or sentence.

### Syntactic

Perhaps the most extensively developed instructional reading procedure related to syntax is that designed by Quigley and King (1980). Although syntax is a level of entry into the decoding of meaning, like GMP it involves a low-level strategy. Limiting the child to syntactic strategies constrains the child's other possible entry efforts. In addition, an emphasis on syntax may cause overattention to form and structure at the expense of meaning, much in the way GMP causes an overfocus on sound-symbol relationships. The suggestions of Quigley and Power (1978) may be helpful if integrated into the total instructional milieu, but they should be avoided as an exclusive instructional methodology.

Various hypotheses may be formed concerning syntactic information in the sentences in Exhibit 6–1 letter, for example:

$H_1$   The personal nature of the text allows for less formal syntax, such as deletions, incomplete sentences, and so on.

$H_2$   Syntax represented in personal letters may closely approximate spoken language grammar because of the informal nature of the conversation.

$H_3$   Tense is consistent across topics with tense change signaling a new topic (paragraph 2 uses all past tense verbs; paragraph 3 uses present tense in question form).

If one examines the sentences in the Figure 6–1 story, they appear deceptively simple. However the sentence, *Carlos said not one word,* is an extremely complex syntactic structure. In this case, the hypotheses available at the syntactic level would be limited, because the child would most likely be unable to recognize the structure due to complexity and infrequent use.

By rewriting the sentences, as we have illustrated, basic structure equivalent to the child's syntactic sophistication can be retained, but the syntax can be better utilized to provide a more elaborate context.

### Graphomorphophonemic

Current literature provides an abundance of strategies for phonemic recognition, discrimination, and production; but most of these strategies have been relatively ineffective in facilitating reading. Because the GMP component of reading has, in the opinion of these authors, already been overemphasized at the expense of other crucial aspects of reading, little attention will be given to it here. GMP strategies are one means for decoding meaning. They are probably least effective when used alone, but they may be helpful when used in conjunction with the other components of reading. The students who can use a GMP strategy do not need to (Aukerman, 1971), because they already use more effective strategies at a higher level. In instruction, it is important to teach syllabic decoding rather than phonemics, for reasons we have noted elsewhere in this book.

Vocabulary development and recognition in the Figure 6–1 story of Carlos and the watch stresses a phonics-type approach that emphasizes the beginning and ending sounds of words. By addressing new vocabulary from a GMP level, in a way that targets syllables rather than phonemes and combines word meaning in the process, vocabulary words will become more realistic entities.

### Summary

The foregoing discussion would seem to suggest a unit of teaching well beyond the phonemic, syllabic, or word level. However, use of the sentence level as the primary unit accompanying a language experience approach to reading instruction also presents difficulties. The difficulties are related to a lack of knowledge of discourse features and context and to a focus on sentence-by-sentence processing (Wilbur, 1977). There are numerous sentence-level programs available, but little focus has been directed toward pragmatic or text cohesion issues with exceptional children. Bryans (1979) suggests some teaching strategies directed toward demonstrating the importance of a search for meaning beyond sentence boundaries, that is, in discourse; teachers may find these helpful.

Mather (1972) hypothesizes that children will learn to read naturally, as they acquire spoken language, if they are not forced into a sense of failure, which is often precipitated by an emphasis on peripheral skills at the expense of central competence or meaning. Rather than teach reading, she suggests that reading be allowed to happen. She maintains that most early readers learn at home as a consequence of being read to, without any attention to the alphabet or listening skills. The significant prerequisite appears to be language acquisition, which can then be used in learning to read. This means surrounding children with books and many models of written language on which to base later hypothesis-testing behavior. In the use of the systems of language, Kaminsky (1976) points to a basic competence to relate sound and meaning with the emphasis on language competence rather than spoken language performance.

## OTHER ISSUES RELATED TO READING INSTRUCTION

Reading instruction, in addition to a central focus on teaching children to read, has several branching issues that concern teachers. These peripheral issues often cloud the central focus, and professionals lose track of the purpose of reading instruction, the facilitation of the reading process for children. If reading instruction allows the learning of reading to occur, it is very possible that many of these side issues will also be resolved.

### Reading Instruction and Language Arts

It is becoming increasingly evident that a closer interrelation and greater coordination must exist between language arts and reading, in classroom instruction. From an academic point of view, such interaction would be equally beneficial to both areas, providing continuous mutual reinforcement and experience in the child's overall linguistic development and a growing sophistication with written language. Effective reading instruction and student success in the language arts areas are both based on an understanding of language and how it is used. As Hickman (1977) points out, "one does not just read, one reads something" (p. 373). Therefore, it would appear to be a logical assumption, based on the broad psychosociolinguistic view presented here, that reading and language arts are both aimed at the same underlying objectives: the efficient and effective use of written language.

### Reading in the Content Areas

Although treated as separate from reading instruction and different from the reading activities related to instruction, reading in the content areas is a concern of educators. In short, reading is reading, a process of gaining information or conversing with an author, regardless of whether it is listed under the heading of science, social studies, health, or any other content area.

Problems of reading in the content areas may indicate a lack of background and experience or, in other words, a well-defined schema that is related to the topic or format dictated by the particular content area. As we have seen, what a child comprehends depends in part on what the child brings to the reading activity. Reading in the content areas involves the child's integration of new information presented in the text with information already possessed. However, too often it is assumed that a person has a sufficient knowledge base to master reading content merely because that person's reading "skill" level represents a certain grade level.

The literature suggests that readers have a more difficult time extracting meaning if there is an overabundance of new information. Bormuth (1974) warns that we must provide a balance of old and new information to ensure integration of new knowledge. Zutell (1977) suggests that teachers need to determine this factor in the child who has difficulty in a particular content area and to provide materials and activities that will facilitate the "necessary conceptual base, and thus make reading easier" (p. 387).

## Reading Rate

The reading rate is another issue addressed in reading instruction and evaluation; it is considered to be a "skill" or ability of the proficient reader. However, problems arise from the assumption that, if reading rate increases, comprehension will decrease. Professionals address this issue from a standpoint that stresses recoding from one form of language to another, through attention to the GMP level of reading.

K. Goodman (1973) stresses that recoding from the visual to the auditory code is ineffective for experienced and rapid readers and thus questions its feasibility for beginning readers. Recoding to the auditory is actually a hindrance to a consistent and rapid reading rate and, according to K. Goodman, should therefore be the final resort for any reader. Kolers (1973) reports from studies conducted with proficient readers that words are regarded as symbols of meaning, and operations occur in terms of meaning and interrelationship with other occurring symbols. He found that the college students who served as subjects for his studies were able to read on an average of 300 words per minute. The maximum rate of letter discrimination is only 30 to 40 words per minute. Therefore he concluded that the readers were not recoding letter by letter or even word by word; if they were, such reading rates would not be possible.

There is an additional important consideration in discussing reading rate. Proficient readers do not employ the same reading rate for all types of reading materials (F. Smith, 1973). The purpose and type of reading should actually govern the speed with which one reads. For example, material for a history exam demands a much slower rate of reading than newspaper comic strips. Although educators are aware that reading rate represents a level of mastery by successful readers, they should also understand that what is necessary is a flexibility in reading rate and a knowledge of when and how such variation should be applied. Reading comprehension is affected by the degrees of speed imposed by the reader. If the speed does not match the material being read, comprehension will suffer. On the other hand, if readers are efficient in dealing with the written message, they will be effective in comprehension.

## Materials for Reading Instruction

In concerns of a peripheral nature that relate to reading, materials for instructional use have probably held the limelight. Materials, as we have seen, have been cited as the cause of both reading failure and reading success. Commercial materials claim that if the teacher uses the materials "correctly," reading success will be almost guaranteed. Such materials have been viewed by both the producers and the consumers as the magic potion of reading mastery. The teacher need only wave a magic wand, namely the materials for reading, in the prescribed manner to accomplish the task of reading instruction. The reading instructional material that commands the greatest allegiance from teachers of reading is the basal reader. In far too many cases, basal readers are employed as the cate-chisms of reading.

Yet what children who are learning to read really need is exposure to the total array of reading material. The demands and experiences of day-to-day reading are not found in basal reader form. Still, LaSasso (1978) reports in her survey of materials and procedures used with hearing-impaired students that "73.5% of the programs . . . use basal readers as either their primary or supplementary approach to teaching reading" (p. 30).

Despite the use of basal readers, reading materials designed to teach reading are not accomplishing that task (Hasenstab & McKenzie, 1981). Quigley, Power, and Steinkamp (1977) note that in the school setting many hearing-impaired students cannot read materials that are necessary for learning. Our own experience attests to the fact that many hearing-impaired children, and also those with normal hearing, are not limited merely in reading-related areas of the academic setting; they also have little facility for the survival, functional, or literary facets of reading outside the educational environment.

What we are suggesting is akin to an individualized approach to reading instruction. In such an approach, materials are selected to accommodate the child; the child is not forced to fit the basal reader or programmed material. As pointed out earlier, children who learn to read before they enter school have learned from the exposure to and use of many different forms of reading material.

**Teachers and Reading Instruction**

We view reading instruction from the standpoint of the model as a basis for instructional and learning strategies. However, as in any learning environment, the teacher is a key factor in fostering effective learning for a child (Hart, 1976). In reading instruction, however, the teacher must not rely on avant garde and faddish materials or band-wagon approaches. Zutell (1977) maintains that, in order to respond to the learning needs of their students, teachers of reading require:

1. an understanding of the reading process as it is practiced by the fluent reader,
2. the knowledge and ability to recognize and distinguish between those aspects of the child's reading performance that mark developmental progress toward fluent reading and those that may be interfering with learning to read,
3. the ability to decide what teacher behaviors will provide the necessary feedback to enable the learner to redirect and reshape reading strategies so that they more closely approximate those necessary for fluent reading. (p. 384)

Teachers must be responsible for preparing themselves to be catalysts in reading instruction. They must do this by acquiring first of all the pertinent knowledge foundation related to the definition, function, and nature of reading as written language. They must be aware of their students and allow them a vast array of reading experiences. They must always be cognizant of available information and the previous knowledge they have acquired and of the areas that will require additional exposure. In reading instruction, teachers must have at their fingertips the wealth of reading materials available, both in the literature and in the functional domain.

**An Environment Conducive to Learning to Read**

Much has been said concerning the importance of a good learning environment, one that will stimulate and motivate a child to absorb knowledge.

The classroom learning environment is a product of the attitudes and practices not only of the teacher directly responsible for educating the child but also of the general school structure and personnel. The attitudes and values fostered by adults in the school setting will have their effect on the students, including the teaching/learning aspects of their reading.

Because most children interpret and enact the values of teachers and others regarding reading, they unconsciously adopt the goals and objectives that have been targeted as important by others. King (1977) accurately observes that "if teachers concentrate on sounding-out words, strive for high test scores, fret over completing all of the pages in a workbook, or make a big thing of checking off skills . . . children will begin to see these as goals of reading" (p. 409).

School practices related to reading instruction can also affect a child's perception of reading and its purpose, function, and place in life. If reading practice emphasizes a 20-minute session held each morning in which small groups of children sit in a semicircle around the teacher and read from "the reading book," the children might well form a rather narrow and possibly distasteful definition of reading.

The time-weary reading group may fail in other ways to provide the climate necessary for beneficial reading instruction. The group session designated as the reading instruction time is too frequently concerned with "skill" development exercises rather than actual reading. This is especially true in the case of poor readers. Yet, as McDermott (1977) observes, these are the very children who need to spend time in reading practice. It is usually the "top" reading group, those who are developing successful reading mastery, who receive reading instruction that truly allows them to practice the reading process.

The environment or stage created by a classroom teacher or reading specialist is symptomatic or descriptive of the philosophies and attitudes fostered not only by the teacher or specialist but also by the school structure they represent. This background can color reading evaluation and instruction and in turn generate the attitudes and goals held by the students and thus affect their success in reading.

## SUMMARY

The instruction of reading, though carried out by educators with the most laudable intent, has too frequently resulted in failure for the students and frustration for the teachers. The definitions, philosophies, and related methodologies that are applied to the reading process with a limited understanding of language and reading as a linguistic function are the root cause of the problem. Perpetuation of the failure and frustration is the fault of the schools themselves, of those responsible for training professionals in the educational field. Yet, there is now a body of psycho-socio-linguistic knowledge with pertinent contributions from various disciplines that needs only to be applied to the teaching of reading in order to improve the situation. This will require alterations in and elaborations of the traditional methods of operation as well as new learning by professionals. The result, however will surely be less faulty intervention, less school failure, and less frustration.

# Chapter 7

# Written Language

*T hey were married and had many children . . .*

On 1965, The little boy was eight years old and he is playing a doll family with the toy furnitures on the table. The teacher is calling a telephone on her desk and she writes with a pen into her note about the telephone numbers at the Kindergarden. She calls it for the department of education. The teacher called to take away for a telephone receiver on the holder and she calls "Goodbye, Mr. secretary!"

The teacher went out of her office and walks in the hall. she goings into the Kindergarden and touch a doorknob, open it. The teacher is standing beyond the door of Kindergarden. She say "Hey, Bobby! are you playing a dolls?" His name was Bobby. he sittings on the chair by the table and he says "Yeah, I do!" The bell is ringing on the wall of kindergarden. It says "Bringinggig! !" The teacher hears it.

Edward S.
3/8/80


## WRITTEN EXPRESSIVE LANGUAGE

The process of language involves two operational directions. One is input, concerned with reception; the other is output, concerned with expression. In spoken language, the primary input avenue is the auditory system, which receives additional contextual support from the other senses. The complementary output or expressive avenue carries speech. These input/output avenues of spoken language are paralleled in written language. The primary modality for reception in written language is vision, while the expressive counterpart is in the motor facility of the hand.

As we have seen, written and spoken languages share the components of language and their respective constraints. However, rule application varies with the code form. Figure 7–1 illustrates the simultaneous inter-relationships and dichotomies. In this chapter, we address the expressive form of written language.

Aside from activities like completing workbook pages, writing spelling or vocabulary words, or copying, writing has traditionally been an area of curriculum reserved for the intermediate and upper educational levels. However, early writing and reading can make a mutual contribution to one another if, as Clay (1977) puts it, the teacher stifles the inclination "to direct, sequence, correct and oversee this learning" (p. 339). Clay suggests that early writing may assist in the visual organization of printed form that is necessary for reading. It also may serve to reinforce hypothesis-testing strategies.

With respect to the writer's perspective, Young and Becker (1965) state that, in undertaking writing, writers must consider what they share and do not share with potential readers. The writer's message or perspective on the topic is presumably an unshared item, or why would the writer be writing in the first place? This is the aspect to be discovered by the reader. The shared items include such things as cultural experiences and, most significantly, the language in which the message is coded. These shared items are the means by which the reader identifies the meaning of the writer's message. The writer makes linguistic choices to convey a message and continues to make a series of choices during the writing that relate to the context and can be discerned by the reader. Elsasser and John-Steiner (1977) describe the task of writing as the unfolding and elaborating, for an

**Figure 7–1** Spoken and Written Language

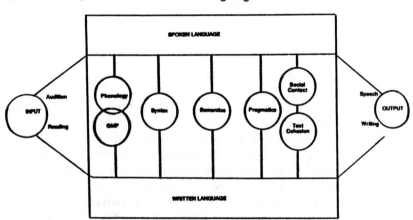

audience that is unknown to the author, those ideas that may be expressed by a word or short phrase in the author's conceptualization.

Writing from the author's perspective involves much more than the mechanics of handwriting, punctuation, capitalization, and spelling—matters that have often been emphasized at the expense of the ability to communicate in writing. Communication in writing can take the form of rhetoric or persuasive writing, descriptive composition, narration, or expository writing. All of these forms require an experiential base, that is, something to communicate or write about.

The many kinds of writing vary from the formal literary form, such as novels, poems, essays, and stories, to less formal types, like that found in conversations, personal letters, and functional communiques, including signs or labels. People write to share information; to persuade; to clarify; to protest; to create; to express thoughts, concerns, and ideas; and to record events and information.

## THE DEVELOPMENT OF WRITING

Between the ages of 3 and 5 years, many children observe that marks made on paper serve a purpose (Clay, 1977) and that written words carry a message or meaning. Another early realization about writing is that what people talk about can be written down. These and other basic ideas about writing may be called *metawriting,* which represents the basic knowledge a child possesses concerning what writing is about.

Children invent writing imitatively by "recording" scribbles across a page (see Figure 7–2). In these early experimental stages of writing, children actually "play" with letter forms. The forms may be rotated or altered in various ways until they lose their identity as letters for the child.

The common starting point of actually producing a meaning representation in print is usually the child's own name (see Figure 7–3). This may be displayed alone or embedded in a combination of other letter forms or miscellaneous markings.

Clay (1977) suggests that, at first, gross approximations of print or script will occur, such as self-designed letters or "make believe sentences" (p. 336) (see Figure 7–4). These efforts, she explains, are the child's request or search for rules of written language in the expressive form. This may be likened to the overgeneralization that occurs in the maturation process of spoken language.

Hildreth (1936) found several stages of writing among young children who had been exposed to print. The process of writing was observed developmentally, ranging from random scribbling, to more refined movement resembling letters, to random letters occurring naturally. There is

**Figure 7–2** Scribbles

(b)

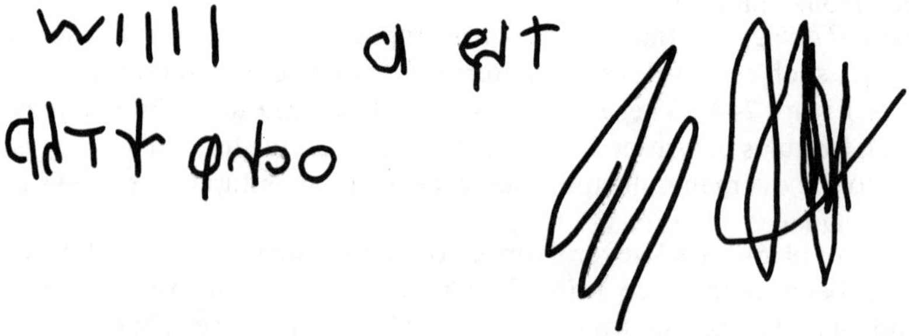

**Figure 7–3** The Child's Own Name

Age 3.4

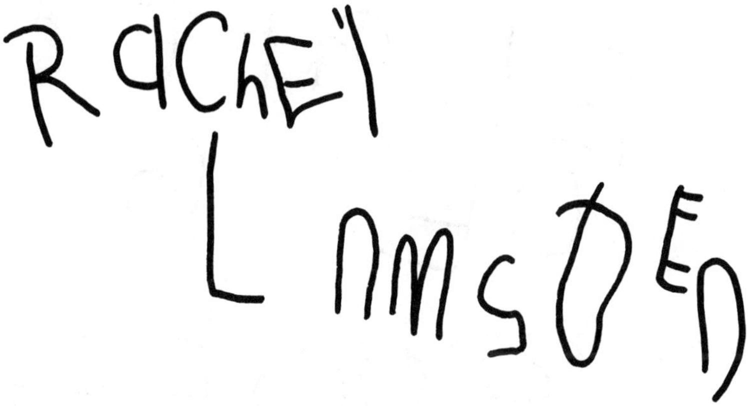

RaCheʼl
Lnmsden

Age 4.4

Jeremy

octavio

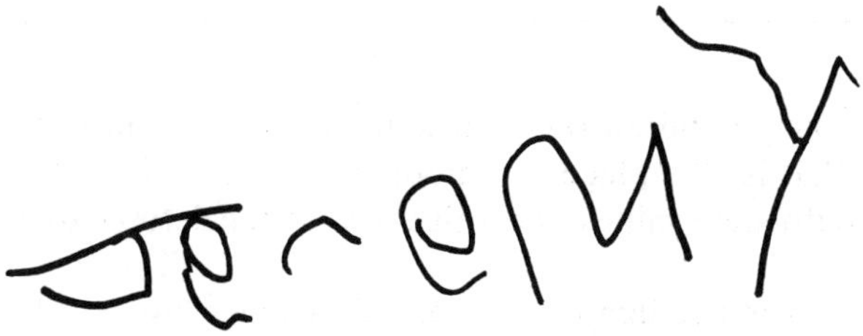

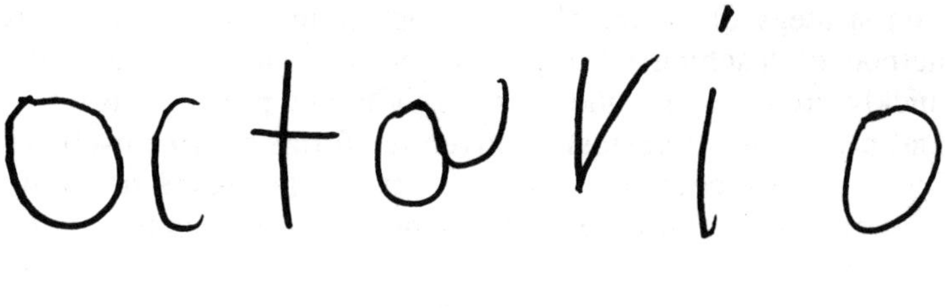

**Figure 7-4**   Make-believe Sentences

Age 4.4

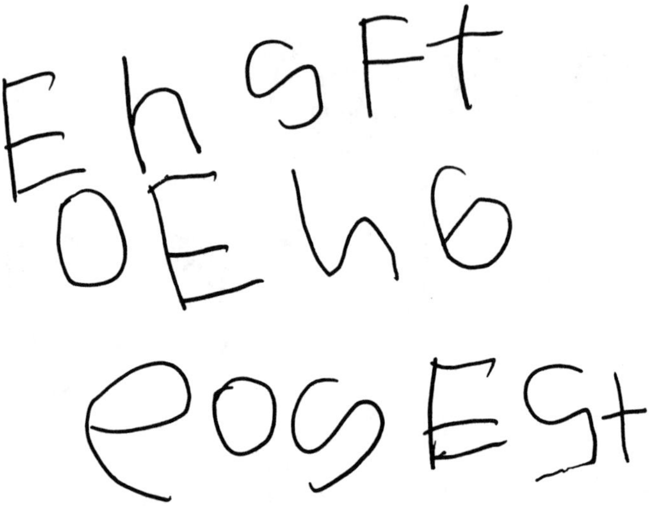

some indication that young children relate articulatory placement to the orthographic system; that is, the place of articulation or how the articulation feels in the mouth determines the selection of the letters to be written.

The phenomenon of overspecification, observed in other areas of linguistic development, may also be noted in the emerging writing of children. The children may insist that their names are their names only when written in a certain way. For example, Sally may say it is her name when it appears in her own form of all capital letters (SALLY) but not when it is put in upper- and lower-case (Sally) or in script *(Sally)*. When children become aware of some rudimentary rules and possess some elements upon which they may impose those rules, they acquire the basis for generating and inventing new operations in writing.

Clay (1977) makes an important observation concerning the commonly used strategy of having children copy letters, words, or sentences as a method of teaching writing at an early stage. She notes that children quickly tire of such "laborious" activity and prefer to turn to "the easier [and more rewarding] task of inventing forms for [themselves]" (p. 337). The urge to record one's ideas or thoughts occurs in many preschool children; but, as in other developmental areas, some children may not display such creative motivation until they have spent some time in school. Whenever this urge occurs, it is important that it be stimulated and fostered, for it is signaling an interest in writing.

Applebee (1977) analyzed the structures used by young children in writing a story. The youngest children produced a series of unrelated statements, while the older children began to sequence events. The episodes of the older children had time order but no central theme. Kretschmer (1979), in analyzing over 3,500 compositions of hearing and hearing-impaired children, found that few hearing-impaired students up to age 18 years could write full complete texts.

As the literature indicates, writing, as in the other aspects of language, is developmental. Children acquire mastery through experience and practice. The initial scribbles become recognizable words that tell a story or give information. Variations in format emerge, and the child writer matures in writing flexibility and facility. This process may be seen in the writing samples of Exhibits 7–1 through 7–7.

**Exhibit 7–1** Letter from Sally

> age 8
> April 22, 1980
>
> Dear Tina,
>
> In school today I'm taking a Reading Test. I have a Lucky Bean. I hope the bean is lucky. Do you think it is?
>
> Your friend,
>
> Sally

**Exhibit 7–2** Story by Sally

> age 9
>
> by Sally
>
> My mother is a teacher. She works with people who can not hear. My Name is Sally. I want to be like her. She teaches people to be like her. She also works with children who cannot hear and have problems with speech. There is a preschool. Lots of children are there. They can't hear and have problems with speech and some do not have any handycap. I'm proud of my mom.
>
> The End

## THE MODEL COMPONENTS APPLIED TO WRITING

As Jenkins et al. (1981) have indicated, written language (text) contains unique features that are not necessary in spoken language, while spoken language has its own unique features not found in written language. These features, while different in form, provide cues for segmentation and old and new information. Syntactic, text-cohesion, and pragmatic cues dominate in discerning meaning in written language; prosodic and nonlinguistic

**Exhibit 7-3**  Essay by Michael

Michael                                                                                  10/1/79
(age 11)
                                    THEME

  Some people have fears, like they fear going in the dark alone or fear of heights and fear of water. These are reasonable fears all right, but talk about a fear! I have this friend that has the wildest fear that I ever heard of. It is fear of being kidnapped by a creature from outer space and taken to a far off galaxy in a suped-up space ship. The guy is so afraid that he won't even whatch TV with anything to do with space or science-fiction.
  It all started two years ago when he saw the film "Close Encounters." Well, when that little boy got picked up, this guy just freaked out and ran out of the theatre yelling, "They'll never take me. If they do it will be over my dead body!" He believes that this secret formula he invented will make him invisible to alien beings. All I have seen it do is make him throw up. Invisible or not the throw-up is a dead giveaway. This may sound strange to some people but the guy thinks this is the real thing. But everyone has different fears that are important to them. So Don't laugh at his fear.
  P.S. this isn't a true story but the point is.

**Exhibit 7-4**  Description of Bell Boys by Chris

Chris
(age 12)
                                   Bell Boys

  Bell Boys carry baggage and escort guests to their hotel rooms. They make sure everything's in order and run errands for thier guests. Bell boys must be neat and courteous and be able to carry heavy bags.
  No education is required but a high school graduation improves chances for promotion. Bell boys and elevator operators don't get promoted very often, usually a couple years when old workers die, retire or leave. They can get promoted to bell captains who are in charge of watching the bell boys and taking complaints from the guests, desk clerks and reservation clerks.

                          Bibliography for Bell Boys
Occupational Outlook Handbook 1978–79 edition.

cues provide such information in spoken language. The types of syntactic structures and even specific lexical selections may, as we have noted, be quite different in written and spoken language. Written language is usually less redundant and more formal and precise and uses different discourse structures, compared with spoken language.

The model components presented in Chapter 3 apply both to the receptive or reading and the expressive or writing aspects of written language. We have already described each of the components and their various strategy or hypothesis domains in the model. Here we will examine how the linguistic components of the model relate to the writings of both normal and exceptional children.

**Exhibit 7–5** Essay by David

David                                                                   9/26/80
(age 13)

    This dilemma centers about when my parents went to a wedding last week. I had a choice of either going to the wedding or working in the yard. So at the time I had a friend over and he said that he would help me move all these rocks from the circle in our driveway to the ditch were I had to make a walkway. So I decided to stay home and work and be board than going to the wedding and be bored. But I should have gone to the wedding, because we were tossing rocks into the ditch and I got hit on the head and ended up with three stitches. Guess that was not so borring after all.

**Exhibit 7–6** Poem by Sumter

Sumter                                                                   4-9-80
(age 14)

Creative Activity

Springtime Cleaning

Spring is Sprung
The flowers bloom
Mom says now
Clean up your room.

Spring is Sprung
I tried my best
But this dumb room
Is still a mess.

Spring is Sprung
And there's no hope
V ith this spring cleaning
I cannot cope.

**Exhibit 7-7** Essay by Chris

---

Chris
(age 15)

Assignment 2840

Sometime way, way back, maybe around the late 1970s or early 80s, people desided that they would repeal the law of gravity and move to a city 5 miles from the face of the earth. Obviously the repeal of the gravity law, known as the Float Act of 1981, would change world wide customs, but I am only here to talk about the Floating City customs of today, 2840.

One major custom is the use of gravity suits, since it is still legal to stand on solid ground. These gravity suits come in a wide variety of colors, like from this end of the rainbow to the other. In These gravity suits you can jump, Float, stand around, fly around among many other fancy tricks.

Some of the other customs are eating breakfast before going to bed to save time in the morning, sneakers, going to work at 9:00, eating lunch at floating restaurants, going home at 5:00, supper, ciggarettes, French fries, hot dogs, cats, beer, microwave everything, TV telephones, spacehouses and birdfeeders.

---

## Writings of a "Normal" Child

The first illustration is that of 5-year-old "normal" Sally. Figure 7–5 shows the story as it was originally written, including Sally's own orthography. For purposes of analysis and reader convenience, the following is a translation into adult spelling:

### When I Woke Up I Was Invisible

Well one day I woke up and
I was invisible and my
mom came upstairs and
called Sally it's time to get up.
Where are you today?

The illustration in Figure 7–6 provides additional information.

Sally's title tells exactly what her story is about. A mini-story format is evident. "One day" sets the scene. The hero or main character in this case is the child herself. The problem is stated immediately by the information, "I was invisible." Then follows a single episode in which the problem is presented and the goal of the story emerges: "My mom came upstairs and called 'Sally it's time to get up.'" But her mother could not find her because she was invisible. Although Sally does not finish her story in written form, her resolution is provided in the accompanying illustration. She explains in her picture that she is invisible.

**Figure 7–5** Story by Sally at 5 Years of Age

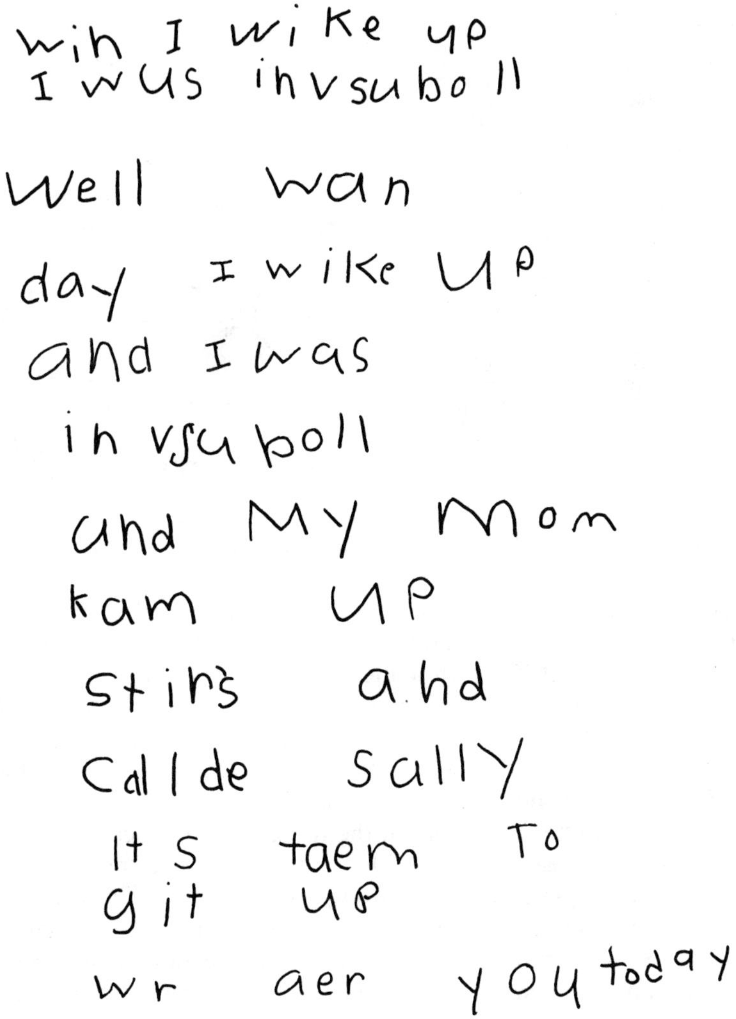

wih I wike up
I wus invsuboll

well     wan

day    I wike up
and I was
  in vsu boll
and My mom
kam    up
stirs    ahd
Callde   sally
  Its  taem  To
git   up
wr    aer   you today

**Figure 7–6** Illustration for Sally's Story

The underlying intent in this case was not to communicate with an audience per se, since the story was written in Sally's personal journal. The child is in fact her own audience. It is interesting and revealing to observe the high level of syntactic structure and lexical selection that the child chose at her own discretion. The word *invisible* is not a typical vocabulary selection that would be made by teachers for a kindergarten child, or even for one in the third grade.

In contrast to her command of the higher linguistic component levels, the unedited Figure 7–5 story shows that Sally has not mastered the conventional English system of orthography. However, in no way has this interfered with her ability to generate the story or with a reader's ability to comprehend her meaning. This raises the question of the necessity of GMP accomplishment as a prerequisite for either reading or writing. It should also be noted that in Sally's story there is no formal punctuation in the form of commas, periods, and so on. She attends to sentence boundaries through the use of space and indicates a new sentence by beginning on another line.

It is apparent that Sally has a command of sophisticated syntactic structure, vocabulary, text cohesion, and pragmatic rules for conveying meaning in story format without previous specific or formalized instruction. Her "instruction" came about through early and constant exposure to reading and writing activity. She had a need and a desire to write, and she had been provided with ample opportunity to observe others at the task and to experiment with the process herself.

As Read (1980) has found in other preschool children, in regard to spelling and the use of orthography, Sally developed through her desire to write her own system of orthography. Although her spellings appear to be errors in English spelling, they are in reality quite explainable and consistent. For further information on what appear to be idiosyncratic but are, in fact, quite systematic spelling systems, the reader is referred to Read's (1980) treatment of preschool English phonology as exhibited in written language. An example of idiosyncratic spelling is shown in Figure 7–7. To our knowledge, there is no linguistic base for this writing.

In contrast to the freedom usually allowed the child writer at home, school writing assignments may dictate the theme or purpose. However, the writer's use of the linguistic components of the model and ever increasing knowledge about writing can still be observed. For example, the essay in Exhibit 7–8 was written by Sally three years later, at 8 years of age. In this example, a growing knowledge about writing form is apparent in that the child is now using an essay format. Yet, it is doubtful that any formal teaching had occurred in the meantime that addressed the difference between the story-grammar and essay form in writing. Sally merely made assumptions and then applied the format based on the purpose of the writing activity as directed by the teacher. It is interesting to note that, in the Exhibit 7–9 essay and in similar writing samples presented in this chapter, the title has been replaced by the child's name and the date. The "body" of the writing then immediately follows.

The purpose of an essay is to present information, which is what Sally does in this sample. The essay format is evident in the presentation of the topic and in the supporting documentation. Sally shows extreme sensitivity

---

**Figure 7-7** An Example of Idiosyncratic Writing and Spelling

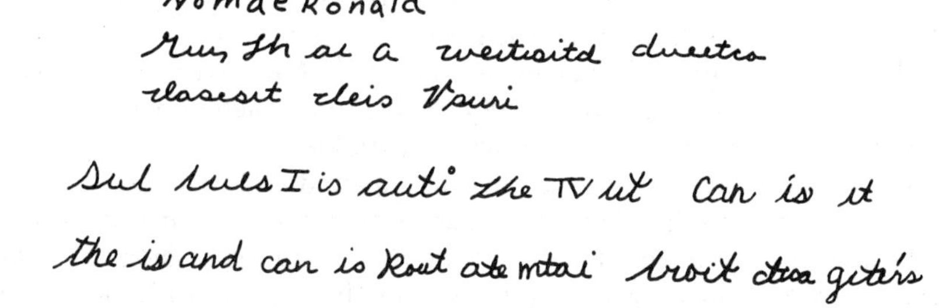

**Exhibit 7–8**  Essay by Sally at 8 Years of Age

| Sally | 4-23-80 |
|---|---|

I'm a bird lover and I know pretty much about birds. One thing I think everybody knows is that a bird lays eggs. Another thing is that a bird lives in a nest and flies. How do birds take off? It's hard to say.

**Exhibit 7–9**  Story by Wendy, a Hearing-Impaired Child

| Wendy | Feb. 22, 1980 |
|---|---|

The man can do magic. He made the broom move by itself. One day a dragon was crying and the man made the dragon better. Now the dragon is the man's best friend. The dragon can ride the man's car. He can make the Hoe cut the cabbage. He has a parrot on the side of the car. The parrot is his pet. The parrot is green, pink, red

*Source:* Laughton & Jones, in progress.

to text cohesion by the manner in which she ties her sentences together. Both anaphoric and cataphoric references (Halliday & Hasan, 1976) as well as tense consistency are in evidence. Sally's pronominalization is consistent, indicating that she has already identified herself by her name. Use of the third person is also consistent throughout the essay.

In the Exhibit 7–9 essay, Sally's mastery of appropriate vocabulary and grammar are apparent. She has incorporated both punctuation and spelling conventions into her writing, although some "misspellings" may still be noted. She has also learned to "self-correct" according to specific conventions of writing, as evidenced by the erasures on her original paper.

### Writings of Hearing-Impaired Children

It has been generally accepted by professionals that hearing-impaired children fail to develop a mastery of writing due to limitations in their auditory abilities and thus in their language systems. Yet, while this may be a basic detriment, it is not insurmountable. Moreover, it does not excuse the fact that limited and faulty exposure through experience and teaching may have helped to perpetuate the problem.

It is our contention that many hearing-impaired children and children with other language-related problems can be taught how to write by utilizing the model components as they relate to written expression, as contrasted with a continuing overemphasis on the aspects of syntax and vocabulary expansion. Exhibits 7–9 and 7–10 present two examples of the writing facility of hearing-impaired students.

In these two cases, the children were shown a film strip depicting a tale about a traveling magician and his performance. The magician manages to seduce a dragon into a partnership. The two samples represent pretests of a study presently in progress (Laughton & Jones, in preparation). No formal teaching of writing was undertaken for either of the children prior to the writing. The samples thus represent what each child learned only through previous informal experience.

In Exhibit 7–9, the story by Wendy (age 10), demonstrates a linguistic competence and a mastery of writing with only slight inaccuracies in text cohesion. For example, she has some difficulty in coding old and new information across sentences. Sentence 1 ("The man can do magic") would more appropriately be in the past tense. In sentence 3, when Wendy abruptly changes the topic (introduces new information) without a cohesive tie, it would have been more appropriate to continue with "the man" as the agent. A further text-cohesion problem arises in Sentences 6 and 7. Although Wendy uses the pronoun "he," the referent is unclear. The reader is unsure as to whether she is using the pronoun to relate to the man or to the dragon.

In other instances, Wendy does use pronouns correctly to refer to old information. The use of text cohesion is seen in Sentence 3, which is tied to Sentence 4 by a time adverbial.

Wendy correctly utilizes the essay format in presenting information about a specific topic. Also, the information is primarily descriptive. Semantically, there is only a little problem in the violation of text cohesion in tying sentences together. Syntactically, Wendy violates the rule for verb + particle in the Sentence 4; the form should be "ride in the man's car" rather than "ride the man's car." She also omits "and" in the descriptive series in the final sentence.

---

**Exhibit 7–10** Story by Patty, a Hearing-Impaired Child

| Patty | February 15, 1980 |
|---|---|

The old man and bird ride on the wagon. And they go empty sand then they show trick. They arrived home. Then man magic on garden near their home and they magic their sofa and chair became fancy pink velvet sofa and chair. They saw dragon was fire all grass. They saw dragon cry and man and bird let dragon to ride on wagon to go different place.

*Source:* Laughton & Jones, in progress.

Like Sally, Wendy had not had any "formal" education in writing. She had, however, grown up since early childhood in surroundings rich in experience with written language. Basically, her expressive writing merely requires some "cleaning up" in the form of teaching and helping her to become aware of more sophisticated strategies in text cohesion.

In contrast to Wendy's writing, Patty's effort in Exhibit 7–10 shows serious violations at all linguistic component levels. Because of the extensive text breakdowns, the reader cannot determine the intent of the author or comprehend the meaning of the passage.

Exhibits 7–11 and 7–12 present aspects that are common in the writing of hearing-impaired students. We would term the type of expression in these samples as "experience chart format." The primary characteristic of this format is the redundant use of the new information topic marker (determiner + noun phrase) with no pronominalization to code old information. Thus, there is no appropriate use of text cohesion to tie the author's thoughts together. The author of the Exhibit 7–12 sample does make some attempt to use pronouns to connect at least two sentences, but he does not carry this through the entire text.

The overemphasis on the the teaching of sentence patterns is shown in these two writing samples. Meaning is forced into a known pattern and thereby stripped of context. The most extreme example of such syntactic constraint might be the following sentence, produced by a 12-year-old boy:

$$\text{``Charlie Brown is real pants.''}$$
$$(NP_1 + be + adj + NP_2)$$

---

**Exhibit 7–11** Passage by Chaiver

Chaiver

> The man is magic.
> He is happy.
> The bird is lying.
> He is car.
> The man is money.
> The moster is cry.
> He is old.
> He is black hat,
> The man is by.

**Exhibit 7–12** Passage by Amy

```
DRGON, 4 film.

                    Drgon is crying.
                    Drgon is ride with man
                    Drgon is not crying again
                    Drgon is happy.
                    man is magic
                    man is ride car.
                    man is happy.
                    man is happy with drgon.
                    man is broom with them.
                    The moster is crying.

                    Amy
                    February 13, 1980
```

## INSTRUCTIONAL STRATEGIES IN WRITING

Shaughnessy (1977) stresses the importance of writing regularly (each day) with few, if any, restrictions of topic, format, and so on. Free writing is necessary to begin the creative process. This is a type of "going through the motions" of writing until the process becomes less difficult and the form of expression becomes more comfortable and familiar. In a sport such as tennis, it is not productive merely to read books about it or to sit and watch tennis matches daily without ever picking up the balls and racquet and actually practicing. Tennis must be practiced; and so it is with writing. Errors are to be expected and indeed can be helpful.

Many commercial writing programs stress the priority of the mechanics of writing. In fact, capitalization, punctuation, and the like are not greatly relevant. It is the message, meaning, and underlying communicative intent that is paramount. This clearly suggests to the teacher that writing without a concern for feedback on technical inaccuracies may in fact be one of the most efficient ways to encourage the emergence of writing with intent or meaning. Teachers should stress the creative aspects of writing and be concerned with low-level corrections later, rather than vice versa as is typically the present situation.

As Moffett (1979) indicates, programs that attempt to teach writing using an elemental or sequential developmental approach are destined to miss the essence of writing text. Many of these programs begin by teaching writing from the word to the sentence to the paragraph to the composition. Only in the complete composition is the total interaction of all the major linguistic subcomponents of written language—texts, cohesion, pragmatics, semantic, syntactic, and GMP—used effectively to convey the meaning. Obviously, the advantages of schema and context are not available at some lower-level writing exercises.

Teachers must abandon the practice of addressing the writing of children in terms of adult priorities. For example, in developing the writing style of children, it would be helpful if the urge of teachers to overstress syntax were suppressed rather than allowed to establish syntax as a central objective. Children should be permitted to feel comfortable in expressing themselves on paper. A teacher who is compelled to apply sentence patterns or rules of capitalization and punctuation can quickly frustrate such expression. Evertts (1970) adds that "overstress on spelling and even on the switch from manuscript to cursive writing, can be similarly inhibiting" (p. 3).

We would endorse Johnson's (1980) guidelines for writing and the reasons for failure experienced by writing teachers. Johnson states that "the emphasis [has been] on 'writing,' rather than on writing—about—something—for—someone. . . . [However] you cannot write writing" (p. 330). The structure of discourse includes the writer, the reader, and the message.

One of the difficulties in learning to write involves the conventions unique to a specific type of text (Hirsch, 1977). These conventions include creation of an implied author with certain intentions and suggested responses for an implied audience. These have been termed the venerable trinity of discourse. Moffett (1980) recommends exposure to a variety of examples from literary and common, daily-living discourse as a basis for writing.

## Examining Objectives in Writing Instruction

### Selection of Topics

For a long time, we have been trying to motivate children to write stories or essays based on what we as adults consider to be interesting to them. We can all recall vividly the dreaded first week of school and the inevitable assignment entitled "How I Spent My Summer." In most cases, summer had been summer; it was over, and now there were hopefully new and exciting avenues to explore. In other words, summer was old information.

Lewis (1970) emphasizes that it is important for children to realize that their ideas are valuable and that they have something to say. Because topics have too often been rigidly imposed by the teacher, many children abandon the hope that they can express their own feelings and thoughts on paper. The objective should be to guide young writers in the expression of self-generated topics. Children do best what they like and like what they do best. This cannot occur if writing is not made enjoyable and comfortable. One's own self is usually the most familiar and comfortable source of ideas.

When writing assignments on a specific topic are made, the students must be provided with a contextual base on which to build their efforts at creative expression. This base should be derived from information on prior and present experiences by pooling such information before the task of writing is undertaken. Even in these instances, however, some freedom of expression should be allowed. For example, the children might be encouraged either to address a preferred aspect of a teacher-selected topic or to write an essay if they prefer.

## Selection of Vocabulary

Too often the richness of meaning that can be portrayed through words is lost in instruction because the children are encouraged to use only those words that they can spell correctly or that are deemed appropriate for their particular grade level. Evertts (1970) cautions that teachers should be careful not to "overdefine" vocabulary words. It is important not to destroy the natural curiosity that children possess for words, their definitions, and their use. For example, children can have an enjoyable time making up their own words.

## Imposition of Syntax

If instruction concentrates too heavily on the structure of sentences and paragraphs, it is easy to lose sight of the fact that meaning is essential in writing. As we have emphasized previously in relation to reading, syntax is a vehicle for the transmission of meaning, not a goal in itself. This applies as well to the role of syntax in writing. Emphasis should be on the use of the many syntactic forms and transformations that the English language has to offer, not on rigid adherence to a finite number of patterns deemed appropriate by a syntactic-based program in language. Teachers must bear in mind the linguistic development of their students and guide them toward flexibility in syntactic complexity.

## Graphomorphophonemic Emphasis

Words are represented lexically or phonetically in orthography (N. Chomsky, 1970). Phonetic differences are represented in such words as *tack* and *pack* where the variation is noted by a different orthographic symbol. Lexical spelling differences are represented in such words as *nation* and *nationality* where the phonetic difference between the first vowel in each word is note by the same orthographic symbol.

In teaching strategies to deal with this type of situation, the teacher should help the writer use not only a phonetic strategy but also a lexical strategy. This requires analysis of root words and word families or, more technically, the internal morphophonemic rules (Vaughn-Cooke, 1977).

We acknowledge that many writers acquire, independently of instruction, successful strategies for correct pronunciation, spelling, and generally for composition. However, our concern is for those who do not successfully develop such strategies. These writers need to use all available strategies, not restricted to a few primitive ones.

Vaughn-Cooke (1977) cites the need for lexical strategies in reading that can apply to writing as well. She uses the example of the word *electricity,* which occurs in a first reader of an early reading program. A lexical strategy that allows the writer to generalize the relationship between *electric* and *electricity* to other analogous words, like *critical* and *criticize,* would greatly help the writer. Such strategies would presumably be effective in both spelling and pronunciation.

**Targets in Teaching Writing**

In selecting objectives for the teaching of writing, educators must be cognizant of the fact that the conveying of meaning is the central goal. Subobjectives in the component areas can assist in this endeavor but they must not override the quest for expression of meaning. The following "targets" in the five component areas of text cohesion, pragmatics, semantics, syntax, and graphomorphophonemics may serve as starting points in developing appropriate objectives in writing instruction:

1. Text cohesion
   - The written paragraph should be the central unit of composition.
   - Paragraphs must be cohesive. This can be accomplished through the understanding and use of pronouns, tense, and other syntactic elements that serve to relate and connect one sentence to another.
   - Text cohesion demands use of vocabulary, sentences, style, logic, and rhetoric in a manner that will allow an audience to understand the writer's message.
   - Outlines in themselves are formats and can be useful in the organization of thoughts and ideas preliminary to actual writing. An outline format should not interfere with creativity; it should enhance it.
   - Writing style and format should be varied with the author's purpose of communication. Practice in the use of a variety of formats will allow children flexibility in written expression.

2. Pragmatics
   - The underlying intent of the author dictates the presentation of old and new information. One alternative is to present initially old information to gather one's audience, then to proceed to new information and its elaboration. Another alternative is to begin with new information. This essentially means starting with the summary.
   - A written conversation requires presuppositions about the reader, the other member of the conversation. This suggests deliberation and decision making by the author regarding his audience.
3. Semantics
   - Children should be encouraged to use new and exciting words in their writing.
   - Meaning is more than a literal translation. Connotative and denotative terms are valuable means of expression.
   - Meaning in the larger sense is the basis of all writing. Young writers need to focus on the meaning they ultimately wish to convey. This is related to and governs purpose.
   - Vocabulary words and spelling lists should not govern word selection.
4. Syntax
   - Sentences are most expressive if varied in complexity and length.
   - A variety of sentence forms allows a writer greater flexibility in expression (there are more sentence patterns than N + V + O).
   - Syntax should be used to organize and cue priorities of information within the sentence. This is accomplished through structures like relative or subordinate clauses.
5. Graphomorphophonemics
   - Correct spelling is a low level priority. The message is the ultimate goal.
   - Spelling expectations should be appropriate to developmental levels of child writers.

**Writing as a Creative Endeavor**

The following "targets" may serve as more general guidelines in developing creative writing:
   - Although the rules of writing related to format, sentences, and so on, are important, teachers must permit young writers to violate such rules (after they have mastered them) in the cause of poetic license.

- Writing requires a realization of audience, which may be self (a diary or journal); a friend (a letter); a person removed by place, relationship, or time (stories, essays); or a large unknown audience (journal articles, books).
- Young writers should be guided in editing their own work. It is more valuable to revise and revamp one's own creation than to have only outside critiques.
- All children are creative, not just the more intelligent ones. However, education often stifles the very children that need the most confidence to exercise their creativity.
- Young writers should be encouraged to write about everything that interests them. Ideas should not be banned or prevented because of teacher inhibitions or goals.
- Teachers should avoid being locked into what we call the red pen correction method. Far too often, a child's writing masterpiece is returned with more red ink than the original blue or black.

**Suggestions for Written Language Instruction**

While they are not meant to serve as specific guidelines or curriculum objectives for written expressive language instruction, the following suggestions may provide a starting point for the generation of teaching strategies. The suggestions are based on the five model components of text cohesion, pragmatics, syntax, semantics, and metawriting in application to written expressive language instruction.

1. Text Cohesion
   - Provide experience and opportunities that allow children to develop recognition for and familiarity with various written formats, such as stories, essays, newspapers, letters, myths, comics, biographies, and fairy tales.
   - Provide experience and occasions that allow children to recognize basic elements of various written formats, for example, story elements of setting, conflict, and resolution.
   - Provide experience and opportunities that allow children to recognize and identify various sources of written communication: books, magazines, newspapers, notes, letters, plays, poetry, and so on.
   - Provide experience and occasions that allow children to recognize and utilize the formats of reference materials, such as dictionaries, encyclopedias, and journals.
   - Provide experience and occasions that allow children to recognize and apply format clues of capitalization, punctuation, paragraph indentation, and so on.

2. Pragmatics
   - Provide experience and opportunities that allow children to recognize and express various intents and forms of expression represented in written language, such as argument, persuasion, answering questions, and information giving.
   - Provide experience and opportunities that allow children to recognize and code old and new information.
3. Syntax
   - Provide experience and occasions that allow children to recognize and apply appropriate grammatical structure and syntax to written language.
   - Provide experience and occasions that allow children to understand and use a variety of sentence patterns.
4. Semantics
   - Provide experience and opportunities that allow children to recognize and use word meaning relative to context rather than merely the dictionary or common definition.
   - Provide experience and occasions that allow children to develop sufficient context for a writing activity before the actual writing is undertaken.
5. Metawriting
   - Provide preschool children and other beginning writers who do not have a basic orientation to writing the experience and opportunity to observe and examine various written materials and writers.
   - Provide opportunities for both "hands-on" experience in investigating writing materials and actual writing experimentation. Specific materials and suggestions for this purpose are presented in Appendix B.

## WRITING AS A MEANS OF EVALUATION

Children's written expressive language may be one of the most valid types of evidence available to evaluate progress in reading and writing (King, 1977). As noted in Chapter 4, rewriting stories as a function of story recall is helpful in the evaluation of comprehension. Such rewriting can also be used in the evaluation of a child's basic knowledge and/or developmental progress in writing.

Children can be read to or told stories or they can read the stories themselves. Analysis based on the model components can then show areas of mastery, areas in development, and target areas for specific instruction.

One difficulty in using writing as a means of evaluation is in determining the appropriate criteria for evaluation. Many criteria for evaluating writing success have been proposed, but a data base for that purpose is lacking.

Diederich, French, and Carlton (1961) and Diederich (1974) distributed 300 papers written by beginning college students to 60 readers in six different occupational areas who then evaluated the merits of the papers. Using various criteria, the readers differed considerably in their evaluations of the papers. Fewer than one-third of the readers regarded the quality of the ideas presented as the major criterion. Usage, sentence structure, punctuation, spelling, wording, and phrasing were all apparently deemed more important than meaning. The same focus appears also to dominate writing or composition instruction in lower-level schools. Professionals thus should be cautioned not to evaluate children's writings based on adult models.

## SPELLING

Most spelling programs are rather highly organized and systematic, sequential attempts to address the underlying assumption that visual discrimination, sound blending, rhyming, sequencing, matching, supplying missing letters, alphabetizing words, and the like are related to an ability to decode the English orthographic-phonologic system. Some attention may be given to the syllable as a unit for attention, but more frequently it is the consonants, digraphs, and vowels that receive attention.

Spelling and the associated writing of words are at best considered by most students to be tolerable exercises. These activities truly represent a drudgery in the academic setting. If it were as difficult to learn to speak words as it is to learn to spell them, we would probably be a less verbal people. In the task of spelling, children, as we have noted, are required to transfer codes or to recode. When a word is pronounced, as in a spelling test, the children must associate the phonemes they hear with the appropriate grapheme representation. Spelling, usually dismissed by educators as easy, is actually a multifactored activity. In explaining spelling complexity, Gudschinsky (1972) states that "the discrete linear nature of the graphic symbols is an artificial abstraction from phenomena which in speech are fused, slurred, simultaneous, and buried within larger structures" (p. 105).

Our present system of writing, together with all of the various conventions it represents, is the product of "arbitrary decisions made during its development by scribes, printers and type setters" (Allen, 1972, p. 90–91). History, as well as an examination of other languages now in use, reveals, for example, that left-to-right progression across the printed page is a hard and fast rule for the presentation of letters and words. The separation of words is another convention that has evolved. Yet, messages composed by the early Greeks and Romans did not contain spacing or other dividing indications. It was not until the 11th century that the convention of word division was established (Allen, 1972).

The English spelling system has come under considerable attack, primarily for failing to be consistent, which is actually a failure to have a one-to-one, grapheme-phoneme match. Chomsky and Halle's (1968) work suggests that the issue is not one of inconsistencies but one of complexity and the failure of most practitioners to understand the English orthographic system. Teachers have always bemoaned the inconsistencies of English spelling, and this has resulted in disparagement of the orthographic system (C. Chomsky, 1980). However, Chomsky and Halle (1968) have pointed out that the spelling of words is more closely related to an underlying abstract level of representation of phonology than it is to the phonetic surface representation of words in spoken language. The rules of the phonological system of language—such as placement of stress and the "phonetic effects of palatization, velar softening, spirantization, voicing, diphthongization, vowel reduction, vowel shift, laxing and tensing of vowels" (C. Chomsky, 1980, p. 54) and the like, which affect abstract lexical representations of syntactic contexts and result in those phonetic forms actually appearing in spoken language—are not well understood by most teachers of reading, writing, and spelling.

In short, lexical spelling, which is akin to the syntactic deep structure, and conventional orthography, which is akin to the syntactic surface structure, correspond with each other but are not identical. That is, "English orthography despite its often cited inconsistencies, comes remarkably close to being an optimal orthographic system for English" (Chomsky and Halle, 1968, p. 49). In other words, "print is more than surface structure" (Allen, 1972, p. 97).

Weir and Venezky (1968) endorse the consistencies and usefulness of English orthography, in which the emphasis is on phoneme and morpheme linguistic aspects rather than on a more simplistic attempt to force a one-to-one sound-symbol correspondence. Those who criticize the orthographic system as being inconsistent, irregular, and a menace to the learning of spelling would be well-advised to look more closely at the literature detailing the complex phonological system that underlies spelling.

C. Chomsky (1980) summarizes the implications of the above view of orthography by noting that the successful reader recognizes the correspondence between abstract lexical spellings of words and the written symbol rather than the simplistic grapheme-phoneme correspondence. Letters represent not sounds but segments of lexical spelling. With respect to instruction, this would suggest the use of word families and a variation of regular pronunciation with individual spelling; that is, how roots change their pronunciation is contingent upon word endings that may be added.

N. Chomsky (1970) is doubtful that a child of 6 years of age has mastered the phonological system, which, he suggests, continues to develop as vocabulary increases and the use of language expands. Therefore, a grapheme-phoneme decoding strategy would appear to be ill-advised either for decoding in reading or for use in spelling. Recommendations for instruction would be best directed toward assisting the child to search for regularities rather than irregularities in the system. It is unfair to burden a child with a strategy that is misunderstood by teachers and therefore unreliable for spelling, for example, the long vowel is followed by the silent *e*. C. Chomsky (1980) has additional suggestions for facilitating spelling that the reader is advised to examine.

Gudschinsky (1972) describes hierarchical strategies for teaching spelling, based on the psycho-socio-linguistic components. She describes development beginning with the level of syllables and morphemes through word level and sentences to the level of pragmatics and discourse. It might be more beneficial to teach children dictionary skills than to try to teach them all of the rules that govern the English phonological-orthographic systems.

Read (1980) points out that the unusual spellings sometimes used by children may actually represent a phonological system of which adults are unaware. This system seems to be based on articulatory features (how the word feels in the mouth when it is said) and is apparent even with preschool children who have had no formal phonological education (Read, 1980). This system could account for such unusual, but consistent, spellings as those found in the writing sample of a 5-year-old shown in Exhibit 7–13.

---

**Exhibit 7–13** Passage by a 5-Year-Old Child

Spring

The bees come uot
side. and the
Flurs come uot, too.
and the sun come
uot too. and The
brdd's come uot too.
and the most thig
wout comes uot
is my cats and
my dog's too.

## SUMMARY

Writing, the expressive form of written language, is a necessary linguistic and creative experience to which all children should be exposed. By guiding rather than imposing adult standards on children's writing endeavors, educators can foster growth in this phase of language and therefore the child's linguistic ability in general.

# Chapter 8

# Notable Quotations on Reading

*A*nd *they lived happily ever after.*

Some of the most revealing insights into the process of reading come from readers themselves. As teachers experienced in the task of teaching reading and in other professional capacities, we believe that selected pieces of wisdom and humor from the readers themselves might serve as a good summary for this book, and perhaps also as a starting point for others engaged in the professional teaching of reading and writing.

In the present chapter, we offer comments from readers concerning reading and its various aspects. Our informal survey of readers posed questions about the nature of reading and how each individual accomplished the task of learning to read. The resulting data provided us with remarkable reinforcement of current psycho-socio-linguistic viewpoints on reading, in addition to many interesting attitudes and opinions about reading instruction and reading disability.

## DEFINITIONS OF READING

The first question we asked was, "What is reading?" The result was a variety of insightful and often humorous responses. Most of the spontaneous definitions related reading to the acquisition of knowledge or to new information. The following are some of the responses:

- "Reading is all the stuff in the whole world." (Joanna, preschool student, age 4)
- "Reading is an avenue of pursuit for those who want to entertain all aspects of life." (Janice, clinical audiologist, age 32)
- "Reading is the gateway to knowledge." (Mary, doctoral candidate, age 34)

- "Reading is what you have to do when you can't figure out any other way to learn." (Mona, superintendent of a school, age 33)
- "Reading is the assimilation of knowledge and interpretation of information from identification of the meaning of symbols inscribed in a pattern meaningful to a particular society." (Donna, assistant professor of education, age 38)
- "Reading is information." (Tony, housing contractor, age 28)
- "Reading is like philosophy: the more you read, the more you learn." (Allegra, reading teacher, age 40)
- "Reading is a form of self-education by which one can go as far as one wishes and travel and experience things you would otherwise never have a chance to do." (John, elementary teacher, age 24)
- "Reading is learnable because it tells you about history and skills to do things and about other countries and some other interesting things." (Sally, fifth grade, age 10)
- "Reading is a skillful way to learn things." (James, fifth grade, age 10)
- "Reading is a complex process by which visual symbols are perceived as words and information in a particular language." (Barry, businessman, age 37)
- "Reading is the understanding of a culture's symbols and language." (Stuart, teacher of social studies, age 26)
- "Reading is what learning is based on and is the most universal source of information." (Wendy, graduate student, age 23)

As we have noted repeatedly, reading success results from a rich background of experience within a linguistic context. Many of our interviews produced definitions of reading as experience oriented. For example:

- "Reading is bringing your background experience to the printed page." (Brenda, university clinical supervisor of language, age 39)
- "Reading is change or potential for change in behavior as a function of written stimuli." (John, professor and chairman, department of special education, age 45)
- "Reading is experience put into words." (Jean, sixth grade, age 11)

Reading was also seen by many respondents to be a source of pleasure. Since motivation and interest are valuable goals and objectives in reading instruction, we felt the following comments were noteworthy:

- "Reading is fundamentally fun." (Nancy, university clinical supervisor in speech pathology, age 27)

- "Reading is getting high on words." (Kim, high school senior, age 18)
- "Reading is the height of vicarious experience." (Wanda, real estate representative, age 35)
- "Reading is therapeutic. It's the great escape from reality." (Zahryl, associate professor of audiology, age 45)
- "It was like kissing the proverbial frog. I was not too enthused at the prospect at first, but I found a whole new adventure opened to me once I had done it." (anonymous, age unknown)

Such commentary on the definition of reading is revealing in that there is little reference to the process as a skill or set of skills that must be accomplished. Rather, reading is viewed by the readers we questioned as experiential and as a major avenue of gaining information. Indeed, the responses describing reading as pleasurable suggest that reading is much more than a functional linguistic process.

## LEARNING TO READ

Reading as a linguistic process is more specifically the receptive aspect of the written and printed form or the visual mode of language. For many readers, written language emerges in much the same manner as spoken language, that is, reading is learned within a sociolinguistic context. Children learn to read by exposing themselves to printed language, by observing reading by others, and by experiencing and practicing reading themselves. For many of the proficient readers we interviewed, reading was not taught through formal instruction. Indeed, it was not uncommon for successful readers to have accomplished the task before they entered school. The following written passages from three children clearly indicate that there was no actual teaching involved in these cases and that their parents were the first source of reading "instruction."

- "How I leaned to read. I Leand to Read like this, my dad and mom red me a book and I looked and thats How I leand to Read."
- "I saw mom, and dad reading all the time. So I started trying and before I new it I could reead then I reed really hard Books and now I am a really good reader."
- "This is how lerned to read. First I took a book and read it and I learnd to read."

King (1977), in her interview with 5-½-year-old Alex presents this insightful recapitulation of early reading accomplishment:

Teacher: How did you become such a good reader?
Alex: I practiced a lot.
Teacher: What do you read?
Alex: Books.
Teacher: Did you say your mother taught you to read?
Alex: No, I did.
Teacher: Did you see anything around that you learned to read from signs or TV?
Alex: No, I just tried reading books.

To determine more specifically how various readers mastered the task of reading, we interviewed colleagues, students, and young acquaintances— all of whom considered themselves "good" readers. To this group we posed the question, "How did you learn to read?" The result was a general consensus that early exposure to printed material was a highly relevant factor. The following are a few of the answers:

- "My mother embroidered the names of the animals on my quilt when I was little. That was my first exposure to words in print." (Frank, university dean, age 50)
- "I had this little black box with letters in it. I used to arrange the letters and pretend they made words and pretty soon they really did." (Tim, associate professor of special education, age 38)
- "I learned to read in Dr. H's preschool. They gave us books and other kinds of reading stuff and we had story time." (Jennifer, kindergarten, age 5)
- "My mother made me read the Bible at about age 4 or 5 or so." (John, businessman, age 24)
- "I learned to read with comic books under the covers with my sister. We used a flashlight. I was 4 and she was 6." (Nancy, speech pathologist, age 27)
- "I learned how to read when I was about four—at home you see. My mom always read to me and the words began to make sense in print." (Sally, fifth grade, age 10)
- "I learned to read before I went to school but I read backwards until I was in fifth grade. Then I figure out words go from left to right the same as sentences." (Rob, high school sophomore, age 15)
- "I just did it." (Sara, teacher of children with learning disabilities, age 40)

- "I learned to read road signs. We travelled a lot when I was little." (Tim, high school freshmen, age 14)
- "My mom read me story books when I was little and when I was about four I started to read back to her." (Becky, sixth grade, age 11)

These selected quotations and many others we gathered illustrate the vital importance of early exposure to reading, not from a structured, formal instructional point of reference, but from natural, spontaneous acquisition based on the linguistic process. Many respondents replied that they had not "learned to read" until they entered school, but they had been read to by their parents before school entry. These respondents said that they had no difficulty in accomplishing the task early in first grade. From this, we can surmise that, although actual reading of sentences and paragraphs may not have been in evidence in preschool, a level of metareading was present that facilitated later success upon school entry. Consider, for example, the following comments:

- "I learned to read in first grade. That seemed to be my main goal 'cause my parents always said, 'You'll learn to really read when you go to school.' I was ready." (Boyd, woodworker, age 30)
- "I used to pretend to read when I was little. I learned to read for real when I went to fist grade." (Natasha, fourth grade, age 9)
- "Last year I was 5 and I knew about books, now I'm 6 and I can read 'em." (Christian, first grade, age 6)

## READING INSTRUCTION

The subject of reading instruction came up frequently in our interviews. Many of the students felt, that although reading itself was pleasurable, the reading materials and instruction failed to motivate and interest them. This view is shown in these candid opinions:

- "Assigned school reading materials violate my good taste. I would rather go to the library." (Mike, high school sophomore, age 15)
- "I think that when they teach reading to kids in school they make it boring and hard, especially for little kids." (Mary, fifth grade, age 10)
- "I really love to read, but prefer my own choices because most school assignments aren't very interesting." (Amy, high school junior, age 16)
- "Mrs.——was my very favoritist teacher 'cause she let us pick any book we wanted. Usually you have just a few picks." (Emily, fifth grade, age 10)

Most of the adults, in reflecting on their school-related experiences, stated that, although they enjoyed reading, many of the circumstances associated with reading lessons were not particularly pleasant. For example:

- "Most things to read in school were boring. I read *Rolling Stone,* comic strips, maps and music instead." (Chris, musician and father, age 20)
- "I could read very well, but not orally. I dreaded being called on to read orally because I knew I would stumble over the words and never know what I read." (Jim, associate professor, special education, age 42)
- "We used to sneak books, like magazines, and comics into class. Really, because what was available was boring to adolescents." (Pat, sales representative, age 30)
- "Reading lessons seemed so stilted with the same procedures every day. At home we were able to read everything." (John, high school mathematics teacher, age 28)
- "Reading group was devastating. Everyone knew the yellow birds were the poorest readers. I was a yellow bird for years, until we quit with the oral reading business." (Manny, associate professor of education, age 45)

Perhaps the following quotations best summarize the difficulties in reading instruction. In our desire to teach children to learn to read, we have inhibited and encumbered the process through overstructure and limitations in materials. "We do not teach children to read, we allow it to occur. The problem is that we have too often been prohibiting rather than allowing" (Barnes' New National Readers, 1884, p. 5).

Yet goals in reading instruction have traditionally focused on the fostering of reading proficiency from a broad perspective. We might speculate from this that reading objectives are often appropriate but that specific methodologies, when applied to the teaching of reading, actually limit or hinder the outcomes the teacher hopes to accomplish. The following excerpt from Spaulding and Bryce (1906) helps to illustrate the intactness and appropriateness of objectives, even from the author's point of view.

A pupil's First Reader should possess these two characteristics: it should be interesting and attractive, and it should serve as the most effective means of teaching the pupil to read independently. That the book be interesting and attractive, from the child's standpoint, of course, it is necessary that the subject-matter be of a kind to appeal to the child. This matter must be chiefly concrete, alive, and active. It must be treated in the language of childhood, and from the child's point of view. The language must present a connected sequence of thought, growing in interest, sentence by sentence, and reaching a distinct climax. And by no means of last importance is the general appearance of the book. That the book present the most effective means of teaching the pupil to read independently, it must be so constructed as to demand or permit such exercises and such applications as lead most rapidly to the mastery of the so-called mechanics of reading. In other words, it must embody a "system," or "method," if we will understand by these terms only an orderly and effective way of doing what must be done in some way. Interest and attractiveness, on the one hand, and system and method, on the other, are characteristics very difficult of combination in a child's first book in reading. The very ideas are more or less antagonistic. Several years' apparently successful effort to combine these ideas practically in scores of classrooms has produced this book. Thousands of children have shown intense interest in the subject-matter here presented, and they have learned to read independently in an almost incredibly short time by the method employed. One will readily form for himself an opinion concerning the merits of the book in respect to attractiveness and interest. The method is not much in evidence to the casual examiner; indeed, it interferes in no way with the use of the book as a "supplementary" reader. Attention is barely called here to only two of the most significant features of the method. (p. v)

The importance of objectives in reading instruction is further illustrated by the "purposes of lessons" presented in *Barnes' New National Readers* (1884):

- To develop the perceptive faculties of pupils by stimulating investigation, the prelude to all accurate knowledge.
- To cultivate the habit of giving written, as well as oral, expression to thought.
- To secure complete and connected statements instead of the rambling modes of expression so common among young pupils.
- To lead the pupil step by step, through the intricate changes of English wordforms, without attempting to teach him the technical terms of grammer.

- To enable the pupil to give the substance of a lesson without entering into tedious and unimportant details.
- To cultivate ease in writing, with pen or pencil, and incidentally to teach the use of capital letters, punctuation marks, etc. (p. 5)

*Barnes' New National Readers* further instruct teachers "not [to] omit poetry. It is no more difficult to read than prose, and far more beautiful" (p. 9). The readers also remind teachers of the importance of reading context: "Remember that example and practice are better than precept and rule" (p. 10).

## READING DISABILITIES

The authors found among the interviewees much interest and concern regarding reading disabilities. On this subject, some of the comments stemmed from the respondents' own experiences or those of their children. Others came from individuals in education or related fields who were familiar with reading problems from their experiences with children with whom they had worked.

One special education teacher succinctly described a reading disability in terms of TV lingo: "A reading disability results in a not-ready-for-prime-time reader." A university professor recalled her dismay when 7-year-old Michael, who had read well before he entered school said, "Hey, Mom, guess what. I'm the smartest kid in the dumb reading group." When the mother asked the reasons for her son's lack of ability in an area in which he had previously performed quite well, the following dialogue ensued:

Child: My teacher said that I can't read.
Mother: That's silly, you could read even before you went to kindergarten.
Child: Yeah, but I don't know the sounds.

This situation is not so uncommon as one may think. For this child and many like him, reading is a recoding procedure based on skill orientation that is debilitating, actually resulting in failure at reading tasks. Even with a child who has previously mastered the process, this can cause dislike for and failure in classroom-related reading instruction. In addition, serious damage can be inflicted on the child's self-perception as a reader. As Michael, now 15 years old, states, "I learned to read when I was four. Then I unlearned it when I was in second grade. I still can't hear individual sounds, but I finally realize that I'm a pretty good reader."

Some of the other interviewees' comments on reading disability are particularly insightful with regard to the nature, cause, and extent of such disability:

- "Reading disability has a cause-effect relationship with school." (Elizabeth, fourth grade teacher, age 36)
- "Reading disability is a distorted view of reading." (Stuart, junior high school teacher, age 26)
- "Reading disability is being in third grade and not having found anything you want to read." (Sarah, third grade teacher, age 40)
- "Reading disability is having words clog up your brain." (Lisa, graduate student in hearing impairment, age 23)
- "Reading means non-sense words." (Susan, graduate student in learning disabilities, age 24)
- "Given that most children learn to talk with little systematic intervention, they obviously receive considerable meddling and misdirection from adults to prevent them from learning to read." (Reg, associate professor of special education, age 49)

## PHONICS

Since phonics is a debatable issue in current psycho-socio-linguistic theory as applied to reading, we asked our audience for their thoughts on the subject. Most responses merely stated that phonics was "sounding out words" and "knowing sounds." In general, phonics was assumed to be part of reading instruction; but, for some, it was not necessarily of value. For example:

- "By the time I sound out the word I forget what I was reading. It's better if I just read over it and get the meaning from what I read." (Lonnie, sixth grade, age 12)
- "It really messes up your spelling." (Sally, fifth grade, age 10)
- "Phonics—Phooey!" (Bill, high school freshman, age 14)

Classroom teachers provided interesting antecdotes from their own experiences in using phonics as an instructional procedure. The following exchange is from a first-grade classroom:

Teacher: Now let's look at this word: Kuh-a-tuh. Who can put the sounds together?
Child: Kuh-a-tuh.

The following exchange was reported from a second-grade classroom:

Child:  Yesterday we learned: h-o-m-e and it said /hom/. Today we learned s-o-m-e and you said its /sum/. How come it's not /som/?
Teacher:  All words are not spelled the way they sound.

Finally, the following dialogue was recorded from a first-grade classroom:

Teacher:  What is this sound?
Child:  duh
Teacher:  OK, now what's this sound?
Child:  uh
Teacher:  Good, and this one?
Child:  kuh
Teacher:  Right, now what's your word?
Child:  I dunno.

## SUMMARY

In this survey, we collected many comments that could not be included here. However, those selected illustrate well the central points presented in previous chapters. It is imperative that we, as educators or other professionals concerned with the acquisition of reading and the attainment of reading success in children, recognize the process for what it is; primarily that of written language. Although written language is not identical with spoken language, it shares psycholinguistic and certain sociolinguistic bases. The view of language as the basis for reading may necessitate alterations in evaluation and instruction. However, by accepting and treating reading as the linguistic process that it is, we may eliminate or at least decrease many of the reading difficulties that children meet in attempting to master the task.

# Diagnostic Reading Tests

Botel Reading Inventory
M. Botel
Chicago: Follett Publishing Company, 1962, revised 1978

*Description*

The Botel Reading Inventory is an informal test intended to supply the classroom teacher with information for determining the child's instructional, independent, and frustrational reading levels. It is also used in the evaluation of knowledge and in determining word recognition skills. The test is designed for use with children in Grades 1–12 and consists of three subtests: (1) Phonics Mastery Test, (2) Word Recognition Test, and (3) Word Opposites Test.

*Technical information*

No normative data are available on how the standards for the reading level classifications were determined. Data on reliability and validity are also lacking.

*Administration and scoring*

The phonics Mastery Test takes approximately 15–25 minutes to complete. It assesses the child's knowledge of consonants, vowels, syllabication, rhyming words, and nonsense words. Scores are determined by summarizing the sound-symbol elements that are in error. No norm tables are presented for this section of the inventory.

The Word Recognition Test contains 20 words at each reading level from preprimer through fourth grade. The child is directed to pronounce words at each level until accuracy falls below 70 percent at two successive levels. The estimated administration time is 4–12 minutes.

The Word Opposites Test is designed to estimate word comprehension. The test may be used as a silent reading comprehension estimator or as a listening potential test. Ten multiple choice alternatives are presented at each level (from first reader through senior high school), and the child is instructed to select a word with the opposite meaning. This section requires approximately 20–30 minutes to administer. The scores obtained serve as a basis for estimating reading levels.

*Summary*

The Botel Reading Inventory suffers severely from a technical point of view. It is probably more realistically appropriate as a criterion-referenced instrument. Item analysis could assist with program-related information.

California Reading Test
E. Tiegs and W. Clark
Monterey, Calif.: California Test Bureau, 1957, revised 1970

*Description*

The California Reading Test, a part of the California achievement test (CAT) series, is a group-administered, norm-referenced assessment tool for measuring student achievement in fundamental reading skills. Each item was chosen for its diagnostic value in measuring achievement in 15 essential elements of reading skills sampled in the subtest sections. There are two forms of the test for each of five educational levels with deliberate overlap at Grades 2, 4, 6, and 9, which permits a continuous score scale from Grades 1–12. The reading test may be used alone or in conjunction with the CAT battery.

| Level 1 | Grades 1 to 2 |
| Level 2 | Grades 2 to 4 |
| Level 3 | Grades 4 to 6 |
| Level 4 | Grades 6 to 9 |
| Level 5 | Grades 9 to 12 |

*Technical information*

The final standardization sample for the CAT (including the California Reading Test) consisted of 203,684 students from 36 states chosen from public school districts and Catholic schools. The sample was selected on the basis of geographic region, average enrollment per grade, and type of community (for public school districts) or type of school (diocesan or private for Catholic schools).

The coefficients of reliability at each level of the California Reading Test are similar. Alternate-form reliabilities reported for the vocabulary and comprehension subtests in the CAT are .84 and .79, respectively. Most researchers have found the reliability to be acceptable. Although the manual of the California Reading Test reports that all levels and forms of the CAT series possess a "high degree of validity," no studies of the validity are presented.

*Administration and scoring*

The manual for the California Reading Test is well-designed with clear and complete directions. A diagnostic profile provided with each test reveals graphically the pupil's achievement for grade placement and age without computation on the part of the teacher. The percentile ranks, grade equivalents, and stanines are well explained, and the scoring is clear. Each item is either right or wrong; no partial credit is given. The score for each section is the number right.

*Summary*

The California Reading Test is believed to be barely adequate for comparing a child's performance in vocabulary and comprehension with the performance of the child's group. Many feel that the subtest scores are too general to be considered diagnostic. The adequacy of the normative sample is difficult to evaluate due to the method of obtaining the selected sample. In addition, norms are based on administration of each level only to appropriate grades. For example, Level 5 was administered to high school students in the sample, but the norms are available down to kindergarten, even though the test was not presented to children at that grade level.

One should be cautious in overinterpreting results found in the very early grades and in overuse of individual-pupil item analysis. In general, this test reveals more in the area of group achievement than it does on the individual child's reading skills and abilities.

Diagnostic Reading Scales
G. D. Spache
Monterey, Calif.: California Test Bureau, 1972

*Description*

The purpose of the Diagnostic Reading Scales is to provide an individualized standardized testing instrument to assess skills in oral reading, silent reading, and auditory comprehension. Designed primarily for use with students at the elementary level (Grades 1–6), it is also suggested for students in higher grades who experience problems or delay in reading. The test is constructed around three main areas:

1. Word lists: Evaluation of word recognition, word analysis. This area presents three word lists of increasing difficulty. There are 130 words in all.
2. Reading passages: Oral and silent reading passages of increasing difficulty, followed by seven or eight questions to determine comprehension.
3. Phonic tests: Eight supplementary subtests designed to tap word analysis skills:
   - Consonant sounds
   - Vowel sounds
   - Consonant blends/digraphs
   - Common syllables/phonograms
   - Blending
   - Letter sounds
   - Initial consonant substitution
   - Auditory discrimination

*Technical information*

The manual does not present any normative data regarding standardization. It does, however, include tables for interpretation of scores.

Reliability data (test-retest), established for the instructional and independent reading levels over intervals from 4 to 10 weeks, and are at .84 and .88, respectively. Internal consistency of the word lists is reported to range from .87 to .96. Reliability information, like normative information, is not presented and is therefore considered insufficient (Salvia & Ysseldyke, 1978).

Validity is also suspect. Although information is presented regarding content and construct validity, it is sketchy and unspecific. Concurrent validity for correlations between the California Reading Test and the Diagnostic Reading Scales is reported to range from .63 to .92. Low correlations of .49 at the independent level and .30 at the instructional level were reported with the reading passages and the Paragraph Meaning Subtest of the Stanford Achievement Test.

*Administration and scoring*

The Diagnostic Reading Scales are individually administered, beginning with the word lists. A child's performance on this scale determines the level to begin the reading passages section of the test. The reading passages scale consists of 22 graduated readings, the results of which are indicative of a student's reading level. Three levels are indicated:

1. an instructional level, relating to materials and classroom instruction levels
2. an independent level, suggestive of recreational reading levels
3. a potential level, an estimate of levels to which a child can feasibly progress after remediation of difficulties

The oral reading passages are also evaluated in regard to errors such as omissions, additions, and substitutions, following the usual format of oral reading tests.

### Summary

Technical information regarding the Diagnostic Reading Scales is lacking. Therefore, caution should be exercised in using the scales. Valuable teaching information may be derived, however, by analysis of student error patterns.

Durrell Analysis of Reading Difficulty
D. D. Durrell
New York: Harcourt Brace Jovanovich, 1955

### Description

The Durrell Analysis of Reading Difficulty has for some time been used as an individually administered, diagnostic reading test. The target population ranges from prereading stages through Grade-6 level. The central purpose defined by the test is to pinpoint reading difficulties for the purpose of remediation. The test is organized around ten subtests that attempt to evaluate oral and silent reading and other related skills. The four primary subtests are:

1. Oral reading: Purpose and procedure are similar to other oral reading tests.
2. Silent reading: Purpose and procedure are similar to oral reading subtest, except that the children read to themselves.
3. Listening comprehension: The examiner reads passages to the child who must answer specific questions regarding the increasingly difficult material.

4. Word recognition and word analysis: Words are exposed for identification via a tachistoscope in a timed (½ second) or untimed presentation. Letters are identified and words "sounded out."

The six supplementary subtests are:

1. Letters: Naming letters presented in print, identifying letters named by the examiner, matching letters that are alike
2. Visual memory of words
3. Sounds: Hearing sounds in words spoken by examiner, learning to have sounds in words, sounds of letters presented in print
4. Learning rate
5. Spelling: phonic spelling of words, spelling dictation
6. Handwriting skills

### Technical information

No information is presented in the test manual relating to standardization, reliability, or validity.

### Administration and scoring

Subtests are administered individually according to manual instructions. A checklist of reading difficulties or instructional needs follows the majority of subtests, which are completed by the examiner. Most of the subtests yield a raw score that may be converted to a representative grade score. The grade level scores may be then charted on a profile.

### Summary

The Durrell Analysis of Reading Difficulty is considered helpful in providing qualitative information that would be useful in developing or altering a student's reading program. Otto, McEnemy, and Smith (1973) support its use except in the case of extensive reading disorders, and Wallace and Larsen (1978) have found it comparable to the Gates-McKillop Reading Diagnostic Tests. However, there is still a question as to whether the Durrell measures reading per se or rather auditory and visual skills and perhaps the ability to answer questions related to a written passage. Once again, caution should be exercised in the interpretation of test results as related to reading as a language function.

Gates-McKillop Reading Diagnostic Tests
A. I. Gates and A. S. McKillop
New York: Teachers College Press, 1962

*Description*

The Gates-McKillop Reading Diagnostic Tests are a battery of 17 individual measures of what the authors regard as reading or reading-related skills. The two forms of the test are designed for use with students in Grades 2 through 6. Areas that are examined by this instrument include:

- Oral reading: Purpose and procedure are similar to other oral reading tests.
- Words—flash presentation: Single words are exposed for one-half second. The purpose is to measure sight vocabulary.
- Phrases—flash presentation: Similar to above subtest but uses short phrases.
- Words—untimed presentation: Word pronunciation. The purpose is to evaluate word attack skills.
- Knowledge of word parts: The purpose is to evaluate word attack skills. There are four aspects of this subtest:

  1. Recognizing and blending common word-parts: Nonsense words are used to determine knowledge of pronunciation rules.
  2. Giving letter sounds: Printed letters must be identified by the corresponding sounds.
  3. Naming capital letters: Upper-case letter forms are identified.
  4. Naming lower-case letters: Lower-case letter forms are identified.

- Visual Form of Sounds: Purpose is to evaluate ability to recode an auditory symbol to visual representation within the context of a word or nonsense word. There are four aspects of this subtest:

  1. Nonsense words: One of four printed nonsense words must be identified as that presented orally by the examiner.
  2. Initial letters: One of four printed letters must be identified as the same as the initial sound in the word presented orally by the examiner.
  3. Final letters: Same as above but for final letter sounds.
  4. Vowels: One of five printed vowels must be identified as occurring medially in a nonsense word presented orally by the examiner.

- Auditory blending: Words are presented orally in parts. The purpose is to determine the ability to blend individual sounds into a word.
- Spelling: Words are orally dictated for the student to write.
- Oral vocabulary: Words are presented orally for the student to define.
- Syllabication: Words are presented for the student to divide into syllables.
- Auditory discrimination: Student must discriminate between common English phonemes. The purpose is to measure discrimination skills, primarily for consonant sounds.

### Technical information

Although the Gates-McKillop test manual presents normative tables, the authors provide no information regarding a normative population. Neither do they provide reliability or validity data for the instrument.

### Administration and scoring

It is not necessary to administer all components of the Gates-McKillop Reading Tests. The individual tests administered to a particular child will depend on the child's age and reading level. The subtests are relatively easy to administer and require little examiner experience. Directions are provided in the test manual, and the student is instructed specifically for each area tested. Performance is recorded in a pupil record booklet that is included in the test.

Although the administration of the test is relatively uncomplicated, scoring and interpretation of test results are difficult and time-consuming. The test manual provides grade score tables from which the examiner can compute raw scores to grade-level representations. Grade scores are determined to be high, medium, low, or very low in relation to the student's grade placement. There are also interpretation tables that compare student performance on the Oral Reading Test with various other subtests. On this basis, the performances are then rated as normal, low, or very low.

### Summary

Despite the obvious limitations of the Gates-McKillop tests—including technical faults, extreme length, difficulty in scoring and interpretation, and the stress on auditory and visual skills rather than on comprehension of information—the instrument is still widely used as a diagnostic test. In fact, it is considered by some to be the most complete diagnostic evaluation instrument commercially available (Wallace & Larsen, 1978). It is, however, questionable whether the test evaluates reading at all. Moreover, extreme caution must be exercised when using a standardized instrument with such a lack of normative data.

Gilmore Oral Reading Test
J. V. Gilmore and E. C. Gilmore
New York: Harcourt Brace Jovanovich, 1968

*Description*

The Gilmore Oral Reading Test is an individual diagnostic test designed to evaluate accuracy, rate, and comprehension in oral reading. It is designed for use with students in Grades 1 through 8.

*Technical information*

The two forms (C and D) of the Gilmore Oral Reading Tests were standardized in 1967 on two normative populations of 2,246 and 2,209 students. The students represented 18 schools and were selected from a variety of socioeconomic areas. However, there is no demographic normative information regarding the students in the sample.

Validity has not been established for the present edition of the test. Limited alternate-form reliability data are presented for 51 students at Grade 3 and 55 students at Grade 6. For Grade 3, coefficients of .94 for accuracy, .70 for rate, and .60 for comprehension in oral reading were reported. For Grade 5, the coefficients were .84 for accuracy, .54 for rate, and .53 for comprehension. Thus, all coefficients except that for Grade-3 oral reading accuracy are below the standard level of .90.

*Administration and scoring*

The two forms of the Gilmore Oral Reading Test contain ten paragraphs that, although arranged in terms of increasing difficulty, present a continuous story form. The student reads each paragraph aloud and responds to oral questions, while the examiner records and scores for accuracy, rate, and comprehension.

Grade and performance scores are presented for accuracy and comprehension of oral reading. Rate does not enter into these scores but is determined to be either "slow, average, or fast." An error analysis is also included with specific examples, description, and explanation provided in the manual.

*Summary*

Technical limitations as well as difficulty in scoring and interpretation of test results suggest that the Gilmore Oral Reading Test should be used cautiously as a diagnostic instrument. The test's systematic analysis of error types might provide the most helpful information, indicating error patterns and strategies used by the student in oral reading.

Gray Oral Reading Test
W. S. Gray and H. M. Robinson
Indianapolis, Ind.: Bobbs-Merrill, 1967

*Description*

The purpose of the Gray Oral Reading Test is to provide an objective diagnostic evaluation of oral reading skills and deficiencies. It was designed for individual use with students from first grade through college. The test purports to assess both speed and accuracy of oral reading.

*Technical information*

Norms for the Gray Oral Reading Test are described by Salvia and Ysseldyke (1978) as "tentative and limited" (p. 173). Original standardization in 1959–1960 was based on 502 children, 40 at each grade level, representing geographical areas of Florida, Chicago, and the Chicago suburban areas. Demographic data are sparse, concerning only sex and geographic location. The authors state that students who demonstrated problems related to health, speech, or emotional difficulty or who had been retained or skipped ahead in school were excluded from the population.

Test validity is based only on opinions derived from data related to a 1915 edition of the test. Reliability information is severely limited, covering only intercorrelations between grade scores on the four test forms. There are no test-retest data presented. Alternate-form reliability coefficients range from .96 to .98 for male students and from .97 to .98 for females.

*Administration and scoring*

The four forms of the Gray Oral Reading Test contain 13 graded passages, each followed by a series of questions to determine comprehension. The student reads each passage aloud and responds verbally to the questions. The examiner records the number and types of errors, reading behavior, and reading time on a student record form.

Beginning levels for testing are indicated in the accompanying manual and are based on the student's grade-level placement. Testing starts with a passage that can easily be read by the student and continues until seven or more errors are observed in two consecutive passages.

Scores are recorded in two ways. First, grade scores indicate a "global" reference for the speed and accuracy of the student's oral reading. The second form of scoring is based on an analysis of error patterns made by the student.

*Summary*

The restricted normative information and the lack of strong validity or reliability data, combined with the difficulty in recording, scoring, and interpreting the Gray Oral Reading Test suggest extreme caution in employing the test's results in diagnostic decisions. Perhaps the most valuable aspect of the test is information from the error analysis. By examining error patterns, the examiner can partially determine oral reading strategies and systematic errors of the student.

Nelson-Denny Reading Test
M. Nelson and E. Denny
Boston: Houghton Mifflin, 1929 (revised 1960, 1965, and 1973)

*Description*

The Nelson-Denny Reading Test, originally developed in 1929, now exists in four forms (A,B,C, and D). Forms C and D were added in 1973 to supplement the 1960 revision. The test evaluates the reading abilities of students in Grades 9 through adult-levels. It consists of four scores: vocabulary, comprehension, reading rates, and a total score.

*Technical information*

A stratified random sampling procedure was used for Grades 9 through 12 to establish a norm for the 1960 version of the test. This norm was based on school enrollment by region and community size (Orr, 1965). The 1973 version has percentile norms for the beginning of the year, the middle of the year, and the end of the year for Grades 9 through 12. The norms for the beginning of the year are empirical norms obtained from the test standardization in October and November of 1972. The other two sets of norms are extrapolated norms. (Forsyth, 1978) The norms for Grades 13 through 16 do not permit much descriptive norm-referenced interpretation of the test scores. Therefore, the college-level norms really do not represent any well-defined population (Forsyth, 1978).

For Grades 9–12, split-half and alternate-form reliability estimates are provided for the vocabulary, comprehension, and total scores. Only split-half estimates are furnished for these three scores at Grades 13 to 16. For

Grades 9–12, only alternate-form reliabilities are given for the reading rate score. No reliability estimates are provided for Grades 13 to 16.

### Administration and scoring

The accompanying manual presents directions for administration and scoring. The vocabulary section consists of 100 multiple-choice questions designed to determine definitions. The reading comprehension section presents 36 questions, also in multiple-choice format. These questions evaluate content in reading passages related to history, economics, literature, sociology, and anthropology. Reading rate is determined by the proportion of a passage read in one minute.

### Summary

Criticism of this test is directed toward the manual and its insufficient information. Norms for the test are limited, and there is a lack of validity and reliability data. Perhaps the greatest problem is in the level of difficulty of the test. Various critiques maintain that it is too difficult for the average high school student.

Phonics Knowledge Survey
D. Durkin and L. Meshover
New York: Teachers College Press, 1964

### Description

The Phonics Knowledge Survey was designed for Grades 1–6. The package includes a content card, a response record, and the test manual. This is a 15-part, individually administered survey, designed to assist teachers in assessing pupil knowledge of phonics. The skills assessed are names of letters; consonant sounds; long and short vowel sounds; vowel generalizations; consonant blend digraphs; vowel combinations (diphthongs and digraphs); vowels followed by /r/; sounds of /qu/, /c/, /g/, /y/, /oo/, and /x/; beginning consonant combinations (digraphs); and sound syllabication.

### Technical information

No norms or data are presented regarding the reliability of validity of the test.

### Administration and scoring

Completion time for the test ranges from 10–30 minutes. The test items become progressively more difficult, and it is suggested in the instructions that the teacher may skip sections that are too difficult for the child. However, it is noted that this does not constitute a partial testing procedure. The examiner checks a "right" or "wrong" response opposite the questions or letters.

## Summary

Although the Phonics Knowledge Survey is designed as a measure of phonics, it is criticized as failing to represent all sounds and overattending to sounds and sound combinations that occur infrequently in written form. The test also suffers technically.

Roswell-Chall Diagnostic Reading Test of Word Analysis Skills
G. Roswell and S. Chall
New York: Essay Press, 1956 (revised 1959)

## Description

The Roswell-Chall Diagnostic Reading Test of Word Analysis Skills was designed to measure basic skills to provide the teacher with an estimate of a pupil's strengths and weaknesses in word recognition.

## Technical Information

Reliability was measured on 52 children receiving remedial reading instruction; a correlation of .98 was found between total scores of Forms 1 and 2. The children ranged from Grade 3 through Grade 11. Reading levels were from Grade 5 through Grade 8, the average being 4.5.

Validity data were based on a sample of two Grade-2 and two Grade-5 classes and on the 52 remedial-level students from the reliability study. Lower validity coefficients were found for the clinic samples than for the other grades, although the test was designed for use with poor readers.

## Administration and Scoring

This individually administered test requires an estimated 5 to 10 minutes to complete. The five subtests evaluate:

1. Ability to determine sounds of consonant letters and consonant blends. All consonants are included except q and x, and there are 10 blends.
2. Knowledge of vowel sounds by determining "short" vowels in isolation, in words, and in sentence context.
3. Awareness of the "silent e" rule.

4. Knowledge of vowel combinations.
5. Mastery of syllabication. There are no tables for interpreting scores for the test. The manual states that, if children miss more than half the items on any subtest, it may be assumed that they have a special deficiency in that area or that they have not received instruction.

## Summary

The Roswell-Chall test may be useful as an informal measure of a child's ability to transfer or recode in sound-symbol relationships. However, there are no technical data for the test, and the normed population sample is a poor one. The short time and ease of administration might be advantageous if the test were used as a quick screening measure.

Silent Reading Diagnostic Tests
J. L. Bond, B. Balow, and C. Hoyt
Ardmore, Pa.: Meredith Corporation, 1970

## Description

The Silent Reading Diagnostic Tests were designed to serve as group-administered tests for use with readers functioning at reading levels between Grades 2 through 6. The authors state that the instrument was designed to evaluate silent reading ability. Actually, the eight subtests assess word attack skills and word recognition. The tests do not provide a means to evaluate comprehension in reading.

The eight skill-oriented subtests are concerned with the following areas:

1. recognition of words in isolation
2. recognition of words in context
3. identification of root words
4. application of syllabication rules
5. sound blending
6. distinguishing initial sounds
7. distinguishing final sounds
8. distinguishing vowels and consonants

## Technical Information

Although the tests were standardized on 2,500 children in 10 cities located in three states, no demographic information on the sample is presented in the manual.

There are no test-retest reliabilities given in the manual, but split-half coefficients ranging from .85 to .97 are reported for the subtests, based on an administration to two fourth-grade classes.

The validity of the tests must be judged in relation to specific reading programs.

*Administration and Scoring*

The authors suggest that the test be administered in three parts, utilizing time periods of approximately 40 minutes. Specific directions for administration and scoring are presented in the manual. Hand scoring keys are also provided.

The subtests yield raw scores that may be converted to grade equivalents, stanines, and percentile ranks and plotted on a student profile chart. Although the profile form designates areas to record vocabulary and comprehension scores, that information must be gained from other evaluation instruments. Raw scores may also be computed to produce an average reading score, which is obviously global in nature. To a limited extent, information regarding error types made by the student may also be derived.

*Summary*

The Silent Reading Diagnostic Tests are quite limited as diagnostic procedures; their results relate only to specific auditory or visual skill information. Failure to define adequately the normative sample makes generalization of the test's scores impossible. It is also questionable whether a global reading "average" provides much pertinent information in program planning and implementation.

Sipay Word Analysis Tests
Edward R. Sipay
New York: Educators Publishing Service, 1974

*Description*

The Sipay Word Analysis Tests are a series of individually administered, criterion-referenced tests devised to diagnose a reader's ability to use decoding skills in the recognition of unknown words. The tests are based on the assumption that reading is an association process and that the child recognizes words by visual analysis, phonic analysis, and visual blending. The series consists of a survey test and 16 additional tests that are to be used selectively as indicated by the results of the survey test. The battery covers the phonic and structural analysis skills usually taught in the primary grades.

## Technical Information

Sipay states that these word analysis tests are criterion referenced. He feels that the tests possess content validity because they measure the skills needed to decode words that are not recognized by sight. Reliability is said to be achieved by providing at least three different items for each symbol-sound association that is sampled. However, no specific data are presented regarding either validity or reliability.

## Administration and scoring

The manual presents descriptions of the skills measured, indicates when to administer a particular test, and provides directions for administering the tests, recording responses, scoring, and interpretation and for follow-up testing suggestions. The individual report forms detail specific strengths and weaknesses, performance objectives, analysis of performance, trial teaching, and follow-up testing suggestions for each skill. The 16 specific tests measure word analysis skills with respect to initial and final consonant blends, digraphs, final silent /e/ generalization, vowel sounds of /y/, letter names, and substitution of single letters. Administration time is estimated at 10 to 20 minutes per test.

## Summary

The Sipay Word Analysis Tests are well-prepared diagnostic measures of word analysis ability. The content is effectively sequenced with a systematic arrangement of stimuli. It must be noted, however, that the tests measure a child's ability to recognize unknown words out of context; the use of words in isolation prevents the child from using content as a clue to word recognition. Sipay also uses artificially divided words in some tests, which does not represent the processing of words in normal reading situations. The manual discusses at greath length visual analysis, phonic analysis, and visual blending; but the tests can be criticized as to whether or not they adequately measure these skills.

Stanford Diagnostic Reading Test
B. Karlsen, R. Madden, and E. F. Gardener
New York: Harcourt Brace Jovanovich, 1977

## Description

Designed as a measure of specific reading skills, the Stanford Diagnostic Reading Test (SDRT) differs from most other diagnostic-type tests in that it may be used as a group oriented test, administered by a teacher to an entire class or to a smaller reading group. It may be used as either a norm-referenced or criterion-referenced instrument. The test measures skills on four levels that overlap one another to provide a continuum. Each level has two forms (A and B). The four levels are designated by color codes. The test is designed for use with students from the end of Grade 1 through Grade 12.

The four skill areas covered by the Stanford Diagnostic Reading Test are:

1. Vocabulary:

   • Auditory vocabulary: Requires the identification of synonyms (pictures or words) for words presented by the examiner. This subtest is for the first three levels only.
   • Word meaning: Definitions of words. This subtest is required only at the fourth level.
   • Word parts

2. Decoding:

   • Auditory discrimination: Requires the identification of similar and different sounds in words. This subtest is included only at the first two levels.
   • Phonetic analysis: Requires identification of sound/letter relationships. This subtest is presented at increasing levels of difficulty at all four levels.
   • Structural analysis: Examines the use of syllables, root words, prefixes, and sound blends. This subtest is used only at the upper three levels.

3. Comprehension:

   • Word reading: Word recognition. This subtest occurs only at the first level.
   • Reading comprehension: Varies at each level with increasing difficulty, from matching sentences and pictures to literal comprehension to inferential comprehension using paragraph format.

4. Rate: Evaluates skill at reading easy material rapidly and the ability to scan printed material. This subtest is included only in the two upper levels.

## Technical Information

Although age and sex were not controlled in the standardization of the SDRT, socioeconomic status, geographic region, and school-system enrollment were. A stratified random sampling technique was employed. Normative data in the manual are extensive, based on 31,000 students in 55 school districts.

Criterion-related validity correlation coefficients between the SDRT subtests and the reading subtest of the Stanford Achievement Test are reported to range from .61 to .98 for the first two levels and from .39 to .94 for the third level. The authors state that content validity must be based on the degree to which the test represents the content of local school curricula.

Alternate-form reliability coefficients for raw scores on the SDRT are reported to range from .75 to .94. Interval-consistency coefficients, reported for all subtests, exceed .90, except for the auditory vocabulary subtest, for which the range is from .85 to .90. The manual also presents reliability information on the progress indicators.

## Administration and scoring

The specific objectives to be assessed are presented for each subtest. Students are requested to respond to directives by the teacher/examiner and to record appropriate answers in test booklets or machine scorable forms. Because the test's scope is flexible, six different scores are obtainable, each of which may be related to the objectives of the testing. The subtest raw scores may be converted to grade equivalents, percentile ranks, stanines, scaled scores, or progress indicators, which are the criterion-referenced scores. Detailed suggestions for test interpretation are included in the manual.

## Summary

The SDRT has the advantage of flexibility, in that it can serve either as an individual instrument or as a group-administered instrument. Also, it can be used as either a norm-referenced or a criterion-referenced test. The SDRT is well-standardized and appears reliable in the areas it was designed to evaluate. Like other diagnostic reading tests, however, the SDRT adheres to a traditional definition of reading as a set of skills rather than an aspect of language.

Woodcock Reading Mastery Tests
R. W. Woodcock
Circle Pines, Minn.: American Guidance Service, 1973

*Description*

The Woodcock Reading Mastery Tests are designed as an individualized, standardized, diagnostic battery to assess reading skills of students from kindergarten through Grade 12. Although they are norm-referenced tests, the author states they may also be used as criterion-referenced instruments. These are two forms of the battery, each designed to examine five targeted areas:

1. Letter identification: Requires the naming of letters presented in manuscript and cursive form. This subtest consists of 45 items divided into eight categories of increasing difficulty.
2. Word identification: Requires the pronunciation of 150 isolated words arranged in graduated levels of difficulty.
3. Word attack: Requires the use of phonetic and structured analysis to determine the pronunciation of 50 nonsense words arranged in order of difficulty.
4. Word comprehension: Evaluates knowledge of word meaning of 70 words presented in analogy format.
5. Passage comprehension: Requires the student to read silently, then provide an appropriate missing word in a modified cloze procedure. The 85 items increase in difficulty from phrases to detailed paragraphs.

*Technical information*

The Woodcock Reading Mastery Test's normative information is well-presented and complete in explanation and form in the manual. The tests were standardized on 5,252 students from kindergarten through Grade 12 in 50 different school systems. Complete demographic information is provided.

A high degree of variability exists among the individual subtests and alternate forms of the tests. The author presents two types of reliability. Split-half reliability coefficients for Grades 2 and 7 generally range from .83 to .99, with the majority above .90. However, coefficients of .02 and .20 are reported for Grade-7 Forms A and B of the letter identification subtests. Alternate-form, test-retest reliability coefficients range from .16 (Grade 7, letter identification) to .94 (Grade 2, word identification). Complete information tables are presented in the manual.

Woodcock presents data related to content validity based on the procedures used to select the test items. Construct validity is considered to be "over sophisticated." Intercorrelations between subtests are reported to range from .04 to .92. However, this wide variance is to be expected, given the wide developmental range that the test evaluates.

*Administration and scoring*

The test materials are contained in an easel kit with complete directions for each subtest described in the manual and for the items as they are presented. The examiner scores performance in an accompanying test booklet. Administration time is approximately 25 to 30 minutes.

The subtests yield raw scores that may be converted by tables included in the manual to standard scores, percentile ranks, grade equivalents, and age equivalents or scores. A total score is viewed as a general index of reading ability. Woodcock also presents a unique "mastery score" that provides an index of reading ability at various difficulty levels.

*Summary*

The Woodcock Reading Mastery Tests are relatively quick, and easy to administer and score. The advantage of the mastery scale is that it allows the examiner to plot a student's reading ability from relatively easy levels to levels that show difficulty or failure. Use of the tests as a criterion-referenced instrument can provide helpful programming information. The tests appear to evaluate skills related to reading based on traditional views.

# Supplementary Reading and Writing Materials

Curriculum Associates, Inc.
Esquire Road; North Billerica, Md. 01862

1. *Grammar & Mechanics Skills Center: Intermediate,* 1977, No. 944

   A collection of workbooks that develops skills in writing syntactically correct sentences, constructing paragraphs, proofreading, using correct punctuation, recognizing parts of speech, and identifying word origins.

2. *Story Starters—Primary,* 1976, No. 264
   G. Willard Woodruff and George N. Moore

   A set of 32 open-ended situation cards with three to four questions on each card to stimulate creative writing.

3. *Elaborative Thinking—Primary,* 1974, No. CA270.9
   George N. Moore and G. Willard Woodruff

   A set of 32 cards, each containing a sentence or short paragraph followed by a comprehension question. A sample of appropriate answers is included on the back of each card. The set may be used to promote reading, oral language, and written language skills.

4. *Working with Stories,* No. 253
   Beth LaFleur

   A collection of 21 duplicating masters, each containing the beginning paragraph of a story. The paragraph introduces a situation and location to be completed by the student.

Developmental Learning Materials
7440 Natchez Avenue; Niles, Ill. 60648

1. *Oral/Written Language Lab,* 1980, No. 703
   David Ingram, Consultant

   Beginning with a simple structures and progressing through complex structures, this structured and manipulative program teaches the student to create, say, read, and/or write grammatically correct sentences. The vocabulary used is on a third-grade level.

2. *Storytelling Pictures,* 1978, No. 224

   A set of 12 color pictures to promote oral and written language skills.

3. *Storytelling Posters,* 1971, No. 223

   A set of 12 black-and-white pictures to promote oral and written language skills.

4. *Alternative Cards,* 1976, No. 396

   A set of 16 color drawings to promote creative writing. Each picture illustrates a problem situation to be solved.

5. *Creative Story Starters I,* 1980, No. 617
   *Creative Story Starters II,* 1980, No. 618
   Lorna Glant

   Each flipbook provides numerous topics for creative story writing. The student chooses one of 15 cards in each of the following categories: what, who, and where. The information on the chosen cards then becomes the stimuli (i.e., the main idea) for an imaginative story

6. *Reaction Cards,* 1973, No. 240

   Each of six situations is represented by four cards—one base card with the initial situation and three possible reaction cards, each offering a different solution to the problem. The cards may be used as story starters.

7. *Sequential Picture Cards I* (6-card sequence), No. P 127
   *Sequential Picture Cards II* (3-card sequence), No. P 161
   *Sequential Picture Cards III* (6-card sequence), No. P 162
   *Sequential Picture Cards IV* (4-card sequence), No. P 242
   Laura Lehtinen Rogan and Charlotte F. Larson

   These sets of picture cards may be used to develop logic and sequencing skills in addition to serving as creative writing stimuli.

8. *Sequential Strip,* 1975, No. 376

   A set of folding sequential stories without words. Each series of six cards depicts a complete story and may be used for oral and written language stimuli.

9. *Open Sequence Cards,* 1974, No. 313

   This set consists of 18 incomplete sequencing situations of varying degrees of difficulty due to the number and position of the missing pictures. The student selects the card(s) to complete the sequence appropriately.

10. *Written Language Cards,* 1976, No. 339
    *Written Language Cards—Affective,* 1976, No. 397

    Each set contains 10 wipe-off cards with blank dialogue balloons for creative writing.

11. *Logic Cards,* 1979, No. 241

    These 30 cards show adolescents in a variety of situations. Logical thinking and sequencing events are emphasized.


Educational Insights, Inc.
20435 South Tillman Avenue; Carson, Calif. 90746

1. *The Language Arts Box,* 1975, No. 9113

   An activity box of games, activities, and skill builders that focuses on the following: creative writing, organizational aids for creative writing, manipulatives, public speaking, dramatics, radio and television, informational writing, language skills, spelling, vocabulary development, and parts of speech. (Levels 1–6)

2. *Story Sparkers,* 1975, No. 7102

   A set of 50 black-and-white photographs to stimulate creative writing. "Quick sparks" encourage the student to title the picture and to choose an opening sentence, while "long sparks" require the student to complete open-ended sentences focusing on inference and point of view. (Grades 3–8)

3. *Reading for Comprehension Series,* 1977, No. 7105
   Elayne Sidley

   A set of 10 skill series, with each series including 50 graded reading paragraphs in inceasing order of difficulty. Each paragraph includes four multiple-choice questions to develop the following skills: getting the main idea, noting details, drawing conclusions, using context clues, finding the sequence, understanding sentences, finding cause and effect, predicting outcomes, making inferences, and reading phrases. (Levels 2–6)

4. *Write On!* 1974, No. 9125
   *More Write On!* 1975, No. 9140
   Paulette Condos

   Each set contains 50 creative writing story starters for adventure, mystery, fantasy, sports, ecology, and humor.

5. *Creative Writing—The Wild and Woolly West,* 1980, No. 2348
   *Creative Writing—Adventure Island,* 1980, No. 2349
   *Creative Writing—Welcome to the Spook House,* 1980, No. 2347
   Paulette Condos Kappos

   Each book presents 20 possible story lines representing situational problems, humor, conflict, adventure, and so on. A variety of formats for creative writing is used, such as writing letters, answering questions, and writing recipes.

6. *Writing about Holidays and Seasons,* 1981, No. 2282
   *Writing about People and Places,* 1981, No. 2283
   *Writing about Feelings,* 1981, No. 2284
   Rozanne Lanczak

   Each book is designed to encourage creative writing by presenting specific writing assignments with "starter" words or phrases. Open-ended, follow-up activities related to the given topic are also included. (Grades 2–4)

7. *"Re-tell Readers"—Volume I* (2.0–2.5), 1980, No. 2200
   *"Re-tell Readers"—Volume II* (2.5–2.9), 1980, No. 2201
   *"Re-tell Readers"—Volume III* (3.0–3.9), 1980, No. 2202
   *"Re-tell Readers"—Volume IV* (4.0–4.9), 1980, No. 2203
   *"Re-tell Readers"—Volume V* (5.0–5.9), 1980, No. 2204
   Emily Hutchinson

   These readers are designed to give practice in reading comprehension, recall of details, and creative writing. Each book contains five stories. The first page of each story provides the text, while the second and third pages present cartoon interpretations of the story with blank captions and dialogue balloons. The fourth page is a related-activity page to aid in language development, reading comprehension, and reasoning.

Instructo/McGraw-Hill
Paoli, Pa. 19301

1. *Creative Writing Stimulators,* 1974, No. 2212

   An individual learning center that includes a poster with 16 story starters, five imagination stimulators, and two sets of picture cards (fantasy and everyday experience).

2. *Punctuation: Periods, Question and Exclamation Marks,* 1974, No. 2214

   An individual learning center to review, reinforce, and extend final punctuation of sentences. Included are puzzle boards, learning boards, jigsaw puzzles, and duplicating masters.

3. Flannelboard Kits:
   *The Three Pigs,* 1978, No. 152
   *Goldilocks and the Three Bears,* 1978, No. 154
   *Ginger Bread Boy,* 1978, No. 155
   *Little Red Riding Hood,* 1978, No. 156
   *Three Billy Goats Gruff,* 1978, No. 162
   *Hansel and Gretel,* 1980, No. 288
   *Rumpelstiltskin,* 1980, No. 289

   Each kit contains flannelboard props to recreate famous children's classics. Such activities promote recall and sequencing skills.

Frank Schaeffer Publications, Inc.
26616 Indian Peak Road; Palos Verdes Peninsula, Calif. 90274

1. *Creative Writing Activity Cards,* 1974
   Frank Schaeffer

   A set of 42 activity cards for primary-intermediate students to promote writing skills.

2. *Fingerprint Funnies,* 1978, No. 479
   *Schoolhouse Sillies,* 1978, No. 478
   Elaine Pelosi and Joy Patten

   Each book contains 20 comical story starters to stimulate creative writing.

3. *Cartoon Comprehension,* 1980, No. FS–551
   Helene Chirinian

   Amusing stories are told in comic-book format. Comprehension questions and a suggested topic for creative writing are included with each story. (Grades 4–8)

4. *Super Reader,* 1980, No. FS–560
   Barbara Gruber

   A set of 20 reading-writing activities that may be used with any story. The activities reinforce reading comprehension, vocabulary development, phonics, structural analysis, and alphabetical order. (Grades 4–8)

5. *Reading for Meaning (Grades 2–3),* 1979, No. 485
   *Reading for Meaning (Grades 3–4),* 1979, No. 486
   Kaye Furlong

   Twenty short, informative stories of high interest are included in each book. Six comprehension questions follow each story and address these skills: identifying the main idea, locating details, defining vocabulary words, and making inferences.

6. *Wiggles and Squiggles,* 1979, No. FS–513

   Each worksheet contains a simple story for the beginning reader and four comprehension questions. A follow-up art activity serves as a motivator and reinforcer for each story. (Grades 1–3)

7. *Story Sequencing,* 1979, No. FS–467

   A 20-page duplicating book with each page showing four cartoons to number in sequential order. After sequencing the pictures, the student answers two comprehension questions and completes a creative writing activity. (Grades 2–4)

8. *Reading Cartoons,* 1979, No. FS–423
   Susan Ryono

   Using a cartoon format, the 20 stories reinforce comprehension, sequencing, context, recall, and inference skills. The student sequences cartoon captions and answers comprehension questions. A final question usually requires the student to write a story. (Grades 2–4)

9. *Understanding What You Read Gameboards* (Grades 1–2), 1980, No. 933

*Understanding What You Read Gameboards* (Grades 2–3), 1980, No. 934
*Understanding What You Read Gameboards* (Grades 3–4), 1980, No. 935
*Understanding What You Read Gameboards* (Grades 4–5), 1980, No. 936

Each book contains five gameboards, with each gameboard emphasizing one of five skills: identifying the main idea, classifying, sequencing, using context clues, and drawing conclusions.

10. *Multiple Comprehension Skills* (Grades 2–3), 1980, No. FS–3107
    *Multiple Comprehension Skills* (Grades 4–5), 1980, No. FS–3108
    Katherine Vallen

    Each set includes 32 stories designed to reinforce specific reading skills. Four questions follow each story and require the student to identify the main idea, draw conclusions, locate facts, and make associations. A bonus activity stimulates creative writing and thinking.

11. *Sequencing Skills* (Grades 2–3), 1980, No. FS–3109
    *Sequencing Skills* (Grades 4–5), 1980, No. FS–3110
    Katherine Vallen

    Each set of activity cards includes 32 illustrated stories. Five sentences related to each story follow for sequencing.

12. *Drawing Conclusions* (Grades 2–3), 1980, No. FS–3103
    *Drawing Conclusions* (Grades 4–5), 1980, No. FS–3104
    Kathey Paredes

    Thirty-two illustrated and amusing activity cards are contained in each set. The student reads short paragraphs and answers specific questions that focus on making judgments and predicting outcomes.

13. *Getting the Main Idea* (Grades 2–3), 1980, No. FS–3105
    *Getting the Main Idea* (Grades 4–5), 1980, No. FS–3106
    Helene Chirinian

    Imaginative stories encourage the student to identify the main idea of each paragraph. Bonus activities stimulate creative thinking and writing.

Kenworthy Educational Services, Inc.
Buffalo, N.Y. 14275

1. *Creative Dialogue*, 1979, No. 1403
   Nancy Buscaglia

   A set of 12 activity cards with cartoon art for conversational creative writing. The cards encourage the student to create story plots and conclusions. (Levels 4–8)

2. *Stories To Finish: Primary Grades*, 1977, No. 1401
   *Stories To Finish: Middle Grades*, 1977, No. 1402

   Each set contains 24 full color cards presenting ministory plots. The cards provide stimuli for developing skills in writing, speaking, and creative dramatics.

Trend Enterprises, Inc.
St. Paul, Minn. 55165

1. *Shuffle & Sort Cards: Intermediate* (Level 1), 1976, No. T–44
   *Shuffle & Sort Cards: Intermediate* (Level 2), 1976, No. T–442

   Each set contains eight four-card stories with humorous, full-color illustrations and amusing dialogues for intermediate readers. The pictures develop logic, sequencing, and organizational skills.

2. *Just Imagine*, 1972, No. T–600

   A set of 12 full-color illustrations designed to develop critical thinking skills in writing.

3. *Finger Puppets—Circus Time*, 1975, No. T–351
   *Finger Puppets—Animal Brigade*, 1975, No. T–352
   *Finger Puppets—Fairy Tales*, 1975, No. T–353
   *Finger Puppets—Once upon a Time*, 1975, No. T–350

   Each of the above sets contains 16 finger puppets that may be used in storytelling, creative dramatics, or as story starters in creative writing.

Educational Design Associates
P.O. Box 915; East Lansing, Mich. 48823

1. *Story Stimulus Cards—Unit One*, 1972, No. 101
   *Story Stimulus Cards—Unit Two*, 1972, No. 102

   Each unit contains 12 unique picture situations that provide the basis for creating a story. All pictures may elicit multiple endings.

2. *Caption Cards—Current Affairs Unit,* 1972, No. 131
   *Caption Cards—Humor Unit,* 1972, No. 132
   *Caption Cards—World of Work,* 1973, No. 133

   Each set contains a total of 12 original cartoons without captions to form the basis for varied language and writing activities. The student is encouraged to design a verbal interaction.

3. *Dilemma Cards—A Values Exploration Unit,* 1972, No. 171

   This set of 10 open-ended picture cards is designed for the student to examine alternative solutions to everyday dilemmas. The specific skills developed are: identifying the dilemma, presenting a solution, and providing a rationale.

4. *Around the House—Unit 1,* 1972, No. 121
   *In the Country—Unit 2,* 1972, No. 122

   Each set of multistory sequence cards contains 32 open-ended sequencing pictures.

Prentice-Hall Learning Systems, Inc.
P.O. Box 47X; Englewood Cliffs, N.J. 76320

1. *Story Strips: Produce Your Own* (Grades 3–6), 1977, No. 268
   *Creating Comics with Story Strips* (Grades 4–6), 1977, No. 282
   Joyce Kohfeldt

   Each book includes story strips in the format of movie frames to promote the student's use of imagination and creativity. The student completes story lines and adds illustrations.

2. *Ghost Stories for Starters,* 1977, No. 283
   Joyce Kohfeldt

   This book contains incomplete stories in a comic book format. The student completes story lines and adds illustrations. (Grades 4–6)

3. *Primary Creative Writing Activities, 1977, No. 730*
   Megan L. Senini

   A set of 20 duplicating masters with simple story starters and illustrations.

ENRICH, Inc.
760 Kifer Road; Sunnyvale, Calif. 94086

1. *Write Now,* 1979, No. EN 72007
   Carol Staudacher

   These stories and comic strips serve as story starters to stimulate original story endings. Each page reinforces the development of reading comprehension and writing skills. (Grades 1–3)

2. *Far Out Story Starters,* 1979, No. EN 75207
   Carol L. King

   Accompanying each illustration is a narrative that sets the stage, introduces the characters (creatures from outer space), and outlines the beginning of a story plot. Questions follow to provide writing hints. (Grades 1–4)


Milliken Publishing Company
St. Louis, Mo. 63103

1. *Creative Language Projects: Book A* (Grades 1–2), 1973, No. LA 01
   *Creative Language Projects: Book B* (Grades 2–3), 1973, No. LA 02
   *Creative Language Projects: Book C* (Grades 3–4), 1973, No. LA 03
   *Creative Language Projects: Book D* (Grades 4–5), 1973, No. LA 04
   *Creative Language Projects: Book E* (Grades 5–6), 1973, No. LA 05
   Mary Pat Mullaney

   Each book contains 28 duplicating masters that present a variety of short, informal activities for creative expression. The activities include interpreting pictures, naming animals, people, objects, products, and so on; writing cartoon captions, directions, poems, letters, and commercials; finding solutions to problems; designing inventions; evaluating advertisements; and designing games.

2. *Creative Expression* (Lower Primary), 1973, No. DR 01
   *Creative Writing* (Primary), 1972, No. DR 02
   *Creative Writing* (Intermediate), 1972, No. DR 03
   *Creative Writing* (Upper Intermediate), 1972, No. DR 04
   Billy Leon Shumate

   Each book covers 12 topics of special interest. Each topic is presented through two activity pages that stimulate oral and/or written expression. Suggestions for developing related stories are also included in the *Creative Writing* books.

Instructional Fair, Inc.
Grand Rapids, Mich. 49501

1. *Creative Problem Solving—Primary,* 1976, No. 2507
   James D. Hoffman

   This book contains open-ended writing activities that encourage expression of feelings and thoughts on specific concepts and problems about self-concept and value clarification. Brief stories are used to describe the concepts/problems and are followed by questions concerning the story.

2. *Creative Writing—Grade 1,* 1976, No. 2501
   *Creative Writing—Grade 2,* 1976, No. 2502
   *Creative Writing—Grade 3,* 1976, No. 2503
   *Creative Writing—Grade 4,* 1976, No. 2504
   James D. Hoffman

   Each book contains 24 open-ended writing activities related to specific topics of interest.

3. *Sequencing in Reading—Level 1,* 1980, No. 2101
   *Sequencing in Reading—Level 2,* 1980, No. 2102
   *Sequencing in Reading—Level 3,* 1980, No. 2103
   *Sequencing in Reading—Level 4,* 1980, No. 2104
   Jackie Swanezy and Anne Vander Velde (Levels 1, 2, 3) Donald Barnes and Arlene Burgdorf (Level 4)

   Each duplicating book provides a broad exposure to sequencing. Activities include sequencing pictured events, words in sentences, sentence fragments, sentences in paragraphs, paragraphs in stories, and events in stories. Other skills include following directions, classifying, predicting outcomes, and identifying cause-effect relationships.

Creative Teaching Press, Inc.
Huntington Beach, Calif. 92649

1. *Make-Believe Story Starters,* 1979, No. CTP 620
   Barbara Fairfax and Sue Parker

   This book of duplicating masters contains 19 story lines for the student to complete. A suggested title, leading questions, helpful words, and illustrations are included to stimulate creative writing. (Grades 1–3)

2. *Desk Top Story Starters,* 1979, No. CTP 619
   Mary Lou Alsin

   This book stimulates creative writing by supplying cut-out props for the student to make related to the given topic. Leading questions and helpful words are also included. (Grades 1–3)

3. *Beginning Writing,* 1979, No. CTP 621
   Mary Lou Alsin and Jana Alsin

   This booklet encourages creative writing by requiring the student to color, cut, and paste together puzzles. The puzzle then becomes the story stimulus. Titles, leading questions, and helpful words are included with the puzzles. (Grades K–2)

4. *Story Sequencing,* 1979, No. CTP 622
   Donna Cabrera

   The student sequences six to eight pictures to make a story. Each story is related to a special monthly happening. If desired, the student may also supply the story's text to stimulate creative writing. (Grades 2–3)

5. *Story Starters—Primary Level,* 1972, No. CTP 104
   *Story Starters for Special Days—Primary,* 1975, No. CTP 106

   Each collection of 50 activity cards encourages creative storywriting by providing plot situations, suggested vocabulary, and related illustrations.

6. *Flub Stubs,* 1975, No. CTP 142
   Cheryl Brown

   This set contains 67 prescriptive task cards, each of which guides the student in correcting a specific error often made in creative writing (i.e., capitalization, punctuation, verb agreement, plurals, word usage, homonyms, handwriting, and composition). After completing a given task, the student is then given a related assignment in creative writing.

Incentive Publications, Inc.
Box 12522, Nashville, Tenn. 37212

1. *Skillstuff, Volume 1* (Reading), 1979, No. IP–79X
   Imogene Forte

   An activity approach to diagnostic/prescriptive instruction in basic reading skills: (1) word recognition, (2) word usage,

(3) comprehension, and (4) reading study. The volume includes model activities, lesson plans, worksheets, and competency reviews.

2. *Skillstuff, Volume 2* (Writing), 1980, No. IP–803
   Imogene Forte and Joy MacKenzie

   An activity approach to diagnostic/prescriptive instruction in basic writing skills: (1) using words and phrases, (2) technical writing, (3) composition and original writing, and (4) writing for everyday living. The volume includes model activities, lesson plans, worksheets, and competency reviews.

3. *Cornering Creative Writing,* 1974, No. IP–099
   Imogene Forte, Mary Ann Pangle, and Robbie Tupa

   Presents 52 learning centers, games, and activities for elementary classroom students.

Learnco Incorporated
Exeter, N.H. 03833

*Writing About Things,* 1977
Gene Oshana

This program examines four basic themes to elicit oral and written language: (1) movement, music, and dramatics; (2) creative activities; (3) storytelling; and (4) social studies and science. These themes are the basis for the 48 illustrated and self-explanatory activity cards. The illustrations and open-ended questions on each card may be used as "starters" for discussion or written assignments. Follow-up and supplementary activities are suggested in the teacher's guide.

Pitman Learning, Inc.
6 Davis Drive; Belmont, Calif. 94002

1. *Storytelling,* 1981, No. 4473–9
   Jean Marzollo

   This book encourages oral and written language development by requiring the student to supply the text. Three sections are included: (1) tell-a-story, (2) nursery rhymes, (3) fairy tales and finger puppets.

2. *Creative Writing in the Classroom,* 1968
   Carol Standacher

   This volume contains basic information about teaching students to write stories and poetry. Ideas for creative writing projects are also included.

Basic Learning Corporation
Williamsville, N.Y. 14221

*Composition Skills—Set A* (Grade 3), 1979, No. BLC 2201
*Composition Skills—Set B* (Grade 4), 1979, No. BLC 2202

Each set contains eight creative writing story starters, each of which has been carefully designed and illustrated. Specific grammar skills (i.e., capitalization, punctuation, etc.) are also addressed by each "starter."

Wise Owl Publications
Los Angeles, Calif. 90028

*Imagine and Write,* 1974, No. 204
Kenneth Maurer

A set of multigraded, wide-ability-range task cards to stimulate creativity and language development through writing and art.

Milton Bradley Company
Springfield, Mass. 01101

1. *Creative Writing Kit,* 1976, No. 7758

   This kit includes activities for combining story elements, word substitution, situation personification, incomplete sentences, and famous letters.

2. *Creative Thinking Pictures,* 1977, No. 7204

   A set of 30 situation pictures that focus on family life and peer relationships, for elementary and junior high school students.

Encyclopedia Britannica Educational Corporation
425 North Michigan Avenue; Chicago, Ill. 60611

*Open Box: Ideas for Creative Expression,* 1977
Martha Hopkins

A language arts kit that promotes language development through the use of multimedia. Activity cards, short strips, and cassettes are included.

The Flaggs, Inc.
P.O. Box 435; Babylon, N.Y. 11702

*Syntactics,* 1973, No. 7395
John Flagg

A gameboard approach to making complete sentences for intermediate and advanced readers.

Carson-Dellosa Publications
P.O. Box 369; Clinton, Ohio 44216

*Cartloads of Creative Story Starters,* 1978, No. CD–005
*Story Starters to "Sharpen" Creative Writing,* 1978, No. CD–015
*Well "Seasoned" Story Starters,* 1978, No. CD–014
Janet Dellosa and Patti Carson

Each book contains word bank story starters—thought provoking and motivating pictures/characters with related word lists—to promote creative writing. Topics include animals, good things to eat, holidays and seasons, occupations, creatures and spooky things, and sports.

The Learning Works
P.O. Box 6187; Santa Barbara, Calif. 93111

*Creative Writing Roundup,* 1976, No. LW 201
*Creative Writing Rocket,* 1976, No. LW 104
Linda Schwartz

Each book contains interesting titles and illustrations to stimulate creativity and to aid the primary/intermediate student in written expression. *Roundup* includes four main sections: story starters, brainstorming, motivators, and poetry. *Rocket* includes five sections: story starters, word starters, picture starters, about me, and learning center writing ideas.

Allyn and Bacon, Inc.
470 Atlantic Avenue; Boston, Mass. 02210

*Evaluating and Improving Written Expression,* 1981
Janice K. Hall

This book presents informal evaluation of writing and activities for teaching writing to students in Grades 4 and above. Activity emphasis is focused on an integrated language arts approach to writing; development of vocabulary, sentence structure, and organizational skills; proofreading and editing skills.

# REFERENCES

Abrahamson, R. An analysis of children's favorite picture story books. *Reading Teacher,* 1980, *33,* 167–170.

Allen, D. What teachers of reading should know about the writing system. In R. Hodges & E. Rudorf (Eds.), *Language and learning to read.* Boston: Houghton-Mifflin, 1972.

Amato, A., Emans, R., & Ziegler, E. The effectiveness of creative dramatics and storytelling in a library setting. *Journal of Educational Research,* 1973, *67,* 161–162, 181.

Anderson, R., & Hidde, J. Imagery and sentence learning. *Journal of Educational Psychology,* 1971, *62,* 526–530.

Anderson, R., & Ortony, A. On putting apples into bottles: A problem of polysemy. *Cognitive Psychology,* 1975, *7,* 167–180.

Applebee, A. A sense of story. *Theory Into Practice,* 1977, *16,* 342–347.

Ashton-Warner, S. *Teacher.* New York: Simon and Schuster, 1963.

Aukerman, R. *Approaches to beginning reading.* New York: John Wiley, 1971.

Barclay, J. The role of comprehension in remembering sentences. *Cognitive Psychology,* 1973, *4,* 229–254.

*Barnes' new national readers* (No. 3). New York: A. S. Barnes Co., 1884.

Bartlett, F. *Remembering.* Cambridge, Mass.: Harvard University Press, 1932.

Becker, W. Teaching reading and language to the disadvantaged—what we have learned from field research. *Harvard Educational Review,* 1977, *47,* 518–543.

Bloomfield, L. Linguistics and reading. *Elementary English Review,* 1942, *19,* 125–130, 183–186.

Bloomfield, L. *Language.* New York: Holt Rinehart and Winston, 1963.

Bond, J., Balow, B., & Hoyt, C. *Silent reading diagnostic tests.* Ardmore, Pa.: Meredith Corp., 1970.

Bormuth, J. The cloze procedure, literacy in the classroom. In W. Page (Ed.), *Help for the reading teacher: New directions in research.* Urbana, Ill.: National Council of Teachers of English, 1974.

Botel, M. *Botel reading inventory.* Chicago: Follett, 1962 (rev. 1978).

Botel, M., & Seaver, J. Literacy plus. In M. Botel (Ed.), *Reading/communication arts resources.* Philadelphia: Botel-Sheppard Associates, 1980.

Broman, B. Story telling: The frosting on the cake. *Childhood Education,* 1975, *51,* 323–324.

Bruner, J., Goodman, J., & Austin, G. *A story of thinking.* New York: Wiley, 1966.

Bryans, B. Breaking the sentence barrier in language and reading instructions. *Volta Review,* 1979, *81,* 421–430.

Burke, C., & Goodman, K. When a child reads: A psycholinguistic analysis. *Elementary English,* 1970, *47,* 121–129.

Bush, C., & Huebner, M. *Strategies for reading in the elementary school.* New York: MacMillan, 1970.

Carlson, K. A different look at reading in the content areas. In W. Page (Ed.), *Help for reading teachers.* Urbana, Ill.: National Conference for Reading Teachers. ERIC Clearinghouse on Reading and Communication Skills, 1975.

Carpenter, P., & Just, M. Sentence comprehension: A psycholinguistic processing model of verification. *Psychological Review* 1975, *82,* 45–73.

Carroll, J. *Language and thought*. Englewood Cliffs, N.J.: Prentice Hall, 1964.

Carroll, J. & Chall, J. (Eds.). *Toward a literate society*. New York: McGraw Hill, 1975.

Chall, J. *Learning to read: The great debate*. New York: McGraw Hill, 1967.

Chomsky, C. Reading, writing and phonology. In M. Wolf, M. McQuillan, & E. Radwin (Eds.), *Thought and language/language and reading*, Harvard Educational Review Report Series No. 14, Cambridge, Mass.: Harvard University Press, 1980.

Chomsky, N. Phonology and reading. In H. Levin & J. Williams (Eds.), *Basic studies in reading*. New York: Basic Books, 1970.

Chomsky, N. & Halle, M. *The sound pattern of English*. New York: Harper & Row, 1968.

Clark, H. & Clark, E. *Psychology and language*. New York: Harcourt Brace Jovanovich, 1977.

Clark, H. & Haviland, S. Psychological processes as linguistic explanation. In D. Cohen (Ed.), *Explaining linguistic phenomena*. Washington, D.C.: Hemisphere Publishing Co., 1974.

Clay, M. A syntactic analysis of reading errors. *Journal of Verbal Learning and Verbal Behavior*, 1968, *7*, 434–438.

Clay, M. Exploring with a pencil. *Theory Into Practice*, 1977, *16*, 334–341.

Cohen, A. Oral reading errors of first grade children taught by code emphasis approach. *Reading Research Quarterly*, 1975, *10*, 616–650.

Dale, P. *Language development, structure and structure* (2nd ed.). New York: Holt, Rinehart and Winston, 1976.

Daniels, J. & Diack, N. *The royal road readers*. London: Chatto and Windus, Ltd., 1962.

DeLawter, J. The relationships of beginning reading instruction and miscue patterns. In W. Page (Ed.), *Help for reading teachers*. Urbana, Ill.: National Conference on Research in English, ERIC Clearinghouse on Reading and Communication Skills, 1975.

Diederich, P. *Measuring growth in English*. Urbana, Ill.: National Council of Teachers of English, 1974.

Diederich, P., French, J., & Carlton, S. Factors in the judgments of writing ability. *Educational test service research bulletin*. Princeton, N.J.: Educational Test Service, 1961.

Doman, G. *How to teach your baby to read: The gentle revolution*. New York: Random House, 1964.

Durkin, D., & Meshover, L. *Phonics knowledge survey*. New York: Teachers College Press, 1964.

Durrell, D. *Durrell Analysis of reading difficulty*. New York: Harcourt Brace Jovanovich, 1955.

Elsasser, N., & John-Steiner, V. An interactionist approach to advancing literacy. *Harvard Educational Review*, 1977, *47*, 355–369.

Emery, D. *Teach your preschooler to read*. New York: Simon & Schuster, 1975.

Evertts, E. (Ed.). *Explorations in children's writings*. Champaign, Ill.: National Council of Teachers of English, 1970.

Farr, B. Oral language competence and learning to read. *Viewpoints*, 1972, *48*, 41–49.

Flesch, R. *Why Johnny can't read—and what you can do about it*. New York: Harper & Bros., 1955.

Forsyth, R. Nelson-Denny Reading Test: A review. In O. K. Buros (Ed.), *The eighth mental measurement yearbook*. Highland Park, N.J.: Gryphon Press, 1978.

Franks, J., & Bransford, J. Memory for syntactic forms as a function of semantic context. *Journal of Experimental Psychology,* 1974, *103*, 1037–1039.

Fries, C. *Linguistics and reading.* New York: Holt, Rinehart, and Winston, 1963.

Fries, C., Fries, A., Wilson, R., and Rudolph, M. *Merrill linguistic readers.* Columbus, Ohio: Charles E. Merrill, 1966.

Garrison, S., & Heard, M. An experimental study of the value of phonetics. *Peabody Journal of Education,* 1931, *9,* 9–14.

Gates, A., & McKillop, A. *Gates-McKillop reading diagnostic tests.* New York: Teachers College Press, 1962.

Gibson, C., & Richards, I. *The language through pictures series.* New York: Washington Square Press, 1959.

Gibson, E. & Levin, H. *The psychology of reading.* Cambridge, Mass.: MIT Press, 1975.

Gilmore, J., & Gilmore, E. *Gilmore oral reading test.* New York: Harcourt Brace Jovanovich, 1968.

Goldberg, H., & Schiffman, G. *Dyslexia—problems of reading disabilities.* New York: Grune & Stratton, 1972.

Goodman, K. A linguistic study of cues and miscues in reading. *Elementary English,* 1965, *42,* 639–643.

Goodman, K. Reading: A psycholinguistic guessing game. *Journal of the Reading Specialist,* 1967, *6,* 126–135.

Goodman, K. Oral reading miscues: Applied psycholinguistics. *Reading Research Quarterly,* 1969, *5,* 9–30.

Goodman, K. Psycholinguistic universals in the reading process. In F. Smith (Ed.), *Psycholinguistics and reading.* New York: Holt, Rinehart and Winston, 1973.

Goodman, K., & Burke, C. *Theoretically based studies of patterns of miscues in oral reading performance: Final report* (Project 9-0375, Grant No. OEG-0-9-320375-4269). Washington, D.C.: Department of Health, Education, and Welfare, 1973.

Goodman, K., & Niles, O. *Reading process and program.* Champaign, Ill.: National Council of Teachers of English, 1970.

Goodman, Y. Using children's reading miscues for new teaching strategies. *Reading Teacher,* 1970, *23,* 455–459.

Goodman, Y., & Burke, C. *Reading miscue inventory: Manual procedure for diagnosis and remediation.* New York: MacMillan, 1972.

Gormley, K., & Franzen, A. Why can't the deaf read? *American Annals of the Deaf,* 1978, *123,* 542–547.

Gray, W., & Robinson, H. *Gray oral reading test.* Indianapolis: Bobbs-Merrill, 1967.

Gudschinsky, S. The nature of the writing system: Pedagogical implications. In R. Hodges and E. Rudorf (Eds.), *Language and learning to read, what teachers should know about language.* Boston: Houghton-Mifflin, 1972.

Guthrie, J. & Tyler, S. *Cognition and instruction of poor readers.* Newark, Del.: International Reading Association, 1977.

Guttman, J., Levin, J., & Pressley, M. Pictures, partial picture and young children's oral prose. *Journal of Educational Psychology,* 1977, *69,* 473–480.

Hallahan, D., & Kaufman, J. *Introduction to learning disabilities: A psycho-behavioral approach.* Englewood Cliffs, N.J.: Prentice-Hall, 1976.

Halliday, M., & Hasan, R. *Cohesion in English.* London: Longman, 1976.

Halliday, M. A. K. *Learning how to mean.* New York: Elsevier, 1975.

Harris, A. *How to increase your reading ability* (5th ed.). New York: McKay, 1970.

Hart, B. *Teaching reading to deaf children.* Washington, D.C.: A. G. Bell Association for the Deaf, 1978.

Hasenstab, M. S., & McKenzie, C. A survey of reading programs used with hearing impaired students. *Volta Review,* 1981, *83,* 383–388.

Hasenstab, M. S., & Schoeny, Z. Auditory processing. In M. S. Hasenstab & J. Horner (Eds.), *Comprehensive intervention with hearing impaired infants and preschool children.* Rockville, Md.: Aspen Systems Corporation, 1982.

Hay, J., & Wingo, C. *Reading with phonics.* Chicago: J. B. Lippincott Co., 1954.

Heber, R., Barber, H., Harrington, S., Hoffmann, C., & Fallander, C. *Rehabilitation of families at RISK for mental retardation* (Progress report). Madison: University of Wisconsin, Rehabilitation Research and Training Center in Mental Retardation, 1972.

Heilman, A. *Phonics in proper perspective.* Columbus, Ohio: Charles E. Merrill, 1968.

Hickman, J. What do fluent readers do? *Theory Into Practice,* 1977, *6,* 372–375.

Hildreth, G. *Developmental sequences in name writing. Child development,* 1936, *7,* 291–303.

Hirsch, E. *The philosophy of composition.* Chicago: University of Chicago Press, 1977.

Hodges, R. & Rudorf, E. *Language and learning to read.* Boston: Houghton-Mifflin, 1972.

Hood, J. Why we burned our basic sight vocabulary cards. *Education Digest,* 1974, *40,* 60–62.

Howes, V., & Darrow, H. *Reading and the elementary school child.* New York: MacMillan, 1968.

Jenkins, J., & Pany, D. Research on teaching reading comprehension: Instruction variables. In J. Guthrie (Ed.), *Reading comprehension and education.* Newark, Del.: International Reading Associates, 1980.

Jenkins, J., Stein, M., & Osborn, J. What next after decoding? Instruction and research in reading comprehension. *Exceptional Education Quarterly,* 1981, *2*(1), 27–40.

Johnson, W. A structural curriculum in English. In M. Wolf, M. McQuillan, E. Radwin (Eds.), *Thought and language/language and reading,* Harvard Educational Review Reprint Series No. 14. Cambridge, Mass.: Harvard University Press, 1980.

Kaluger, J., & Kolson, C. *Reading and learning disabilities.* Columbus, Ohio: Charles E. Merrill, 1969.

Kaminsky, S. Bilingualism and learning to read. In A. Simoes (Ed.), *The Bilingual Child.* New York: Academic Press, 1976.

Kamm, K. Focusing reading comprehension instruction: Sentence meaning skills. In C. Pennock (Ed.), *Reading comprehension at four linguistic levels.* Newark, Del.: International Reading Association, 1979.

Karlin, R. *Teaching elementary reading: Principles and strategies.* New York: Harcourt Brace Jovanovich, 1971.

Karlsen, B., Madden, R., & Gardener, E. *Stanford diagnostic reading test.* New York: Harcourt Brace Jovanovich, 1977.

King, M. Evaluating reading. *Theory Into Practice,* 1977, *16,* 407–418.

Kintsch, W. *The representation of meaning in memory.* New York: John Wiley, 1974.

Kintsch, W., & Greene, E. The role of culture-specific schemata in the comprehension and recall of stories. *Discourse Processes,* 1978, *1,* 1–13.

Kirk, S. *Educating exceptional children*. Boston: Houghton-Mifflin, 1962.

Kirk, S. Diagnostic, cultural and remedial factors in mental retardation. In S. Osler & R. Cooke (Eds.), *Biosocial basis of mental retardation*. Baltimore: Johns Hopkins Press, 1965.

Kirk, S., & Kirk W. How Johnny learns to read. *Exceptional Children*, 1956, *22*, 158–160.

Kirk, S., Kliebhan, J., & Lerner, J. *Teaching reading to slow and disabled learners*. Boston: Houghton-Mifflin, 1978.

Koblinsky, S., Cruse, D., & Sugawara, A. Sex role stereotypes and children's memory of story content. *Child Development*, 1978, *49*, 452–458.

Kolers, P. Three stages of reading. In F. Smith (Ed.), *Psycholinguistics and reading*. New York: Holt, Rinehart and Winston, 1973.

Kretschmer, R. *Language development in the hearing impaired: Assessment and educational planning needs*. Paper presented at Atlanta Area School for the Deaf, Atlanta, Ga., 1980.

Kretschmer, R., & Kretschmer, L. *Language development and intervention with the hearing impaired*. Baltimore, Md.: University Park Press, 1978.

Kussmaul, A. Disturbance of speech. *Cyclopedia of Practical Medicine*, 1877, *14*, 581–875.

LaSasso, C. National survey of materials and procedures used to teach reading to hearing impaired children. *American Annals of the Deaf*, 1978, *123*, 22–30.

Laubach, F., Kirk, E., & Laubach, R. *The new streamlined English series, teacher's manual*. Syracuse, N.Y.: New Reader's Press, 1967.

Laughton, J., & Jones, G. Sense of story: hearing impaired students. Book in preparation, 1982.

Laughton, J., Jones, G., & McCubbin, M. *Rocking chair studies* (No. 1). Book in preparation, 1982.

Ledson, S. *Teaching your child to read in 60 days*. New York: W. W. Norton & Co., 1975.

Lefevre, C. *Linguistics and the teaching of reading*. New York: McGraw Hill, 1964.

Lewis, R. A vital experience. In E. Evertts (Ed.), *Explorations in children's writing*. Champaign, Ill.: National Council of Teachers of English, 1970.

Liberman, A., Mattingly, I., & Turvey, M. Language codes and memory codes. In A. Melton & E. Martin (Eds.), *Coding processes in human memory*. Washington, D.C.: V. H. Winston and Sons, 1972.

Lipton, A. Miscalling while reading aloud: A point of view. *Reading Teacher*, 1972, *25*, 759–762.

Lowerre, G., & Scandura, J. Development and evaluation of conceptually based materials for diagnostic testing and instruction in critical reading based on logical inference. *Reading Research Quarterly*, 1973–1974. *9*, 186–205.

Mandler, J., & Johnson, N. Remembrance of things passed: Story structure and recall. *Cognitive Psychology*, 1977. *9*, 111–151.

Maranda, E., & Maranda, K. *Structural models in folklore and transformational essays*. The Hague: Mouton, 1971.

Mather, D. The language learner in school. In R. Hodges & E. Rudorf (Eds.), *Language and learning to read*. Boston: Houghton-Mifflin, 1972.

McConnell, F. *Storytelling and myth-making*. New York: Oxford University Press, 1979.

McDermott, R. The ethnography of speaking and reading. In R. Shuy (Ed.), *Linguistic theory: What can it say about reading?* Newark, Del.: International Reading Association, 1977.

McKenzie, M. The beginnings of literacy. *Theory Into Practice*, 1977, *16*, 315–324.

Meyer, B. *The organization of prose and its effect on memory*. Amsterdam: Elsevier North-Holland Publishing Co., 1975.

Moffett, J. Integrity in the teaching of writing. *Phi Delta Kappan*, 1979, *60*, 276–279.

Moore, O. *Autotellic responsive environments and exceptional children*. Hamden, Conn.: Responsive Environments Foundation, 1963.

Moores, D. *Educating the deaf, psychology, principles and practices*. Boston: Houghton-Mifflin, 1978.

Morgan, W. A case of congenital word blindness. *British medical journal*, 1896, *2*, 1376–1379.

Naslund, R., Thorpe, L., & Lefever, D. *The SRA achievement tests*. Chicago: Science Research Associates, 1954 (rev. 1958, 1963, 1978).

Nelson, M., & Denny, E. *The Nelson-Denny reading test*. Boston: Houghton-Mifflin, 1929 (rev. 1960, 1965, 1973).

Nurss, J. Oral reading errors and reading comprehension. *Reading Teacher*. 1969, *22*, 523–527.

Olson, D. From utterance to text: The bias of language in speech and writing. *Harvard Educational Review*, 1977. *47*, 257–281.

Orr, D. Nelson-Denny reading test: A review. In O. K. Buros (Ed.), *The sixth mental measurement year book*. Highland Park, N.J.: Gryphon Press, 1965.

Orton, S. *Reading, writing and speech problems in children*. New York: W. W. Norton & Co., 1937.

Otto, W., McEnemy, R., & Smith, R. *Corrective and remedial teaching (2nd ed.)*. Boston: Houghton-Mifflin, 1973.

Parrill-Burnstein, J. Problem solving and learning disabilities: An information processing approach. New York: Drune and Stratton, 1981.

Pearson, P., & Johnson, D. *Teaching reading comprehension*. New York: Holt, Rinehart and Winston, 1978.

Pearson, P., & Spiro, R. Toward a theory of reading comprehension instruction. *Topics in Language Disorders*, 1980, *1*, 71–88.

Piaget, J. *The child's conception of number*. New York: W. W. Norton & Co., 1952.

Pressley, G. Mental imagery helps eight-year olds remember what they read. *Journal of Educational Psychology*, 1976, *68*, 597–602.

Proger, B., & Mann, L. Criterion-referenced measurement: The world of gray versus black and white. *Journal of Learning Disabilities*, 1973, *6*, 72–84.

Quigley, S., & King, C. *Reading milestones*. Beaverton, Ore.: Dormac, 1980.

Quigley, S., & Power, D., & Russell. The test of syntactic abilities (TSA) syntax program. Beaverton, Ore.: Dormac, 1978.

Quigley, S., Power, D., & Steinkamp, M. The language structure of deaf children. *Volta Review*, 1977, *79*, 73–84.

Quigley, S., Power, D., Steinkamp, M., & Jones, B. *The test of syntactic abilities (TSA)*. Beaverton, Ore.: Dormac, 1978.

Rasmussen, D., & Goldberg, L. *S.R.A. basic reading series*. Science Research Associates, 1965.

Read, C. Preschool children's knowledge of English phonology. In M. Wolf, M. McQuillan, & E. Radwin (Eds.), *Thought and language /language and reading* (Harvard Educational Review Reprint Series No. 14). Cambridge, Mass.: Harvard University Press, 1980.

Richardson, J., Smith, H., & Weiss, B. *The linguistic readers.* New York: Harper & Row, 1965.

Robinson, H. *Why children fail in reading.* Chicago: University of Chicago Press, 1946.

Robinson, H. *Phonics instruction—when, what, for whom? Teaching word recognition skills.* Newark, Del.: International Reading Association, 1971.

Roswell, G., & Chall, S. *Roswell-Chall diagnostic reading test of word analysis skills.* New York: Essay Press, 1956 (rev. 1959).

Rumelhart, D., Notes on a schema for stories. In D. Bobrow, A. Collins (Eds.), *Representation and understanding.* New York: Academic Press, 1975.

Rumelhart, D. Understanding and summarizing brief stories. In D. LaGerge, & S. Samuels (Eds.), *Basic processes in reading: Perception and comprehension.* Hillsdale, N. J.: Lawrence Erlbaum Associates, 1977.

Russell, W., Quigley, S., & Power, D. *Linguistics and deaf children.* Washington, D.C.: A. G. Bell, 1976.

Salvia, J., & Ysseldyke, J. *Assessment in special and remedial education.* Boston: Houghton-Mifflin, 1978.

Salvia, J., & Ysseldyke, J. *Assessment in special and remedial education* (2nd ed.). Boston: Houghton-Mifflin, 1981.

Sanders, D. *Aural rehabilitation: A management model.* Englewood Cliffs, N.J.: Prentice Hall, 1982.

Schoolfield, L., Timberlake, J. *The phonovisual method.* Washington, D.C.: Phonovisual Products, 1960.

Searle, J. *Speech acts.* London: Cambridge University Press, 1969.

Searle, J. Indirect speech acts. In M. Cole and J. Morgan (Eds.), *Syntax and Semantics, 3.* New York: Academic Press, 1975, 59–82.

Sexton, E., & Herron, J. The Newark phonics experiment. *Elementary School Journal* 1928, *28,* 691–701.

Shaughnessy, M. *Errors and expectations: A guide for the teacher of basic writing.* New York: Oxford University Press, 1977.

Shetler, K., & Simon, S. *Storytelling: A participant manual.* St. Augustine: Florida School for the Deaf and Blind, 1980.

Shuy, R. (Ed.). *Linguistic Theory: What can it say about reading?* Newark, Del.: International Reading Association, 1977.

Sipay, E. *Sipay word analysis tests.* New York: Educators Publishing Service, 1974.

Smith, F. *Comprehension and learning.* Toronto: Holt, Rinehart and Winston, 1975.

Smith, F. Making sense of reading and reading instruction. *Harvard Educational Review,* 1977. *47,* 386–395.

Smith, F. Psycholinguistics and reading. New York: Holt, Rinehart and Winston, 1973.

Smith, F., & Goodman, K. On the psycholinguistic method of teaching reading. *Elementary School Journal,* 1971, *71,* 177–181.

Smith, N. *Reading instruction for today's children.* Englewood Cliffs, N.J.: Prentice Hall, 1963.

Snyder, L. Cognitive and communicative abilities and disabilities in the sensorimotor period. *Merrill-Palmer Quarterly,* 1978, *24,* 161–180.

Söderbergh, R. *Reading in early childhood: A linguistic study of a preschool child's gradual acquisition of reading ability.* Washington, D.C.: Georgetown University Press, 1977.

Spache, G., & Spache, E. *Reading in the elementary school* (2nd ed.). Boston: Allyn & Bacon, 1969.

Spache, G. *Diagnostic reading scales.* Monterey, Calif.: California Testing Bureau, 1972.

Spache, G., & Spache, E. *Reading in the elementary school.* Boston: Allyn & Bacon, 1973.

Spaulding, F. E., & Bryce, C. T. *A first reader. The aldine readers.* New York: Newsome Co., 1906.

Spalding, R., & Spalding, W. *The writing road to reading.* New York: Morrow & Co., 1969.

Stark, J. Reading: What needs to be assessed. *Topics in Language Disorders,* 1981, *1,* 87–94.

Stauffer, R. *The language experience approach to the teaching of reading* (2nd ed.). New York: Harper & Row, 1980.

Stewig, J. Storyteller: An endangered species? *Language Arts,* 1978, *55,* 339–345.

Strang, R. *Reading.* Belmont, Calif.: Fearon Publishers, 1968.

Strang, R. *Diagnostic teaching of reading.* New York: McGraw Hill, 1969.

Stratemeyer, C., & Smith, H. *The linguistic science readers.* New York: Harper & Row, 1963.

Sutton-Smith, B. The importance of the storytaker: An investigation of the imaginative life. *Urban Review,* 1975, *8,* 82–95.

Thorndyke, E. Reading as reasoning: A study of mistakes in paragraph reading. *Journal of Educational Psychology,* 1917, *8,* 323–332.

Tiegs, E., & Clark, W. *California reading test.* Monterey, Calif.: California Test Bureau, 1957 (rev. 1970).

Torrey, J. Learning to read without a teacher. *Elementary English,* 1969, *46,* 550–556.

Tuinman, J. Determining the passage dependency of comprehension questions in five major tests. *Reading Research Quarterly,* 1973, *9,* 206–224.

Vaughn-Cooke, A. Phonological rules and reading. In R. Shuy (Ed.), *Linguistic theory: What can it say about reading?* Newark, Del.: International Reading Association, 1977.

Wallace, G., & Larsen, S. *Educational assessment of learning problems.* Boston: Allyn & Bacon, 1978.

Wardbaugh, R. *Reading: A linguistic perspective.* New York: Harcourt, Brace & World, 1969.

Weaver, C. *Psycholinguistics and reading: From process to practice.* Cambridge, Mass.: Winthrop Publishers, 1980.

Weber, R. A linguistic analysis of first grade reading errors. *Reading Research Quarterly,* 1970, *5,* 427–451.

Weiner, M., & Cromer, W. Reading and reading difficulty: A conceptual analysis. *Harvard Educational Review,* 1967, *37,* 620–643.

Weir, R., & Venezky, R. English orthography—more reason than rhyme. In K. Goodman (Ed.), *The psycholinguistic nature of the reading process.* Detroit: Wayne State University Press, 1968.

White, B. *The first three years of life.* Englewood Cliffs, N.J.: Prentice Hall, 1975.

Wilbur, R. An explanation of deaf children's difficulty with certain syntactic structures of English. *Volta Review,* 1977, *79,* 85–93.

Wisher, R. The effects of syntactic expectations during reading. *Journal of Educational Psychology,* 1976, *68,* 597–602.

Wolf, T. Reading reconsidered. *Harvard Educational Review,* 1977, *47,* 411–429.

Woodcock, R. *Woodcock reading mastery tests.* Circle Pines, Minn.: American Guidance Service, 1973.

Young, R., & Becker, A. Toward a modern theory of rhetoric: A tagmemic contribution. *Harvard Educational Review,* 1965, *4,* 450–468.

Zintz, M. *The reading process: The teacher and the learner.* Dubuque, Iowa: William C. Brown, 1980.

Zutell, J. Teacher informed response to reader miscue. *Theory Into Practice,* 1977, *16*(5), 384–391.

# Index

## A

Abilities
  *See also* Skills
  auditory, 44
  auditory/vocal, 61
  linguistic-reasoning, 83
  oral reading, 60
  vs. performance, 68
  reading, 65
  reasoning, 83
  visual, 44
  vocal, 61
Abrahamson, R., 90
Academic functioning, 63
Accent, 15
Access to words, 22, 23
Achievement
  reading, 63
  testing of, 63-64, 65
Acquisition
  of articulation, 55
  of language, 45, 70
  of vocabulary, 110
Acuity, 68
Allyn and Bacon, Inc., 197
Alsin, Jana, 194
Alsin, Mary Lou, 194
*Alternative Cards,* 184
Amato, A., 96
American English sound system

complexity, 13
Analysis
  grapheme-phoneme, 85
  miscue, 73, 74, 76
  for new word determination, 18
  phonetic, 61
  semantic, 54
  structural, 61
  syntactic, 49
  task, 65
  word, 60, 61, 64, 168
  written language sample, 75
Anaphoric references, 25, 76, 136
Applebee, A., 129
Argument, 6
  format of, 23
*Around the House,* 191
Articles, 55
Articulation, 53
  acquisition of, 55
Ashton-Warner, S., 17
Associations
  *See also* Relationships
  auditory, 44
  consonant sound-vowel sound, 17
  letter-sound, 17, 61
  sound-symbol, 18
  visual, 44
  word-picture, 64
At risk, defined, 42
Attention

instruction, 117
Individual tutoring, 26
Inference, 95
Inferential comprehension, 62
Information, 48
  auditory, 56
  coding of, 137
  new. *See* New information
  old. *See* Old information
  overabundance of, 115
  processing of, 29
  sequencing of, 55
Informative function of language, 55
Ingram, David, 184
Initiative, 17
Input/output avenues of spoken
  language, 123
Insertion, 60
Inside-out processing. *See* Top-down
  processing
Instruction
  goals of, 158, 159
  individualized approach to, 117
  materials for, 116-117
  reading, 95-97, 116-117, 157-160
  storytelling as focus for, 95-97
  and teachers, 117
  writing, 140-142, 144-145
Instructional Fair, Inc., 193
Instructional materials, 69
Instructional strategies in writing,
  139-145
Instructo/McGraw-Hill, 187
Instrumental function of language, 54
Instruments for evaluation. *See* Tests
Integrated use of linguistic strategies,
  33
Intelligence, 29, 68
  operationalized definitions of, 28
  tests of, 65
Intelligibility of speech, 55
Intent
  of author, 47, 48
  communication of, 56
Interactions
  as function of language, 54

spontaneous, 47
Interest, 44
Internalization of visual representation,
  61
Internal morphophonemic rules, 142
Interpersonal communication, 23
Intersentence relationships, 27
*In the Country,* 191
Intonational patterns in spoken
  language, 109
Inversion, 60
Isolated subskills, 45

## J

Jenkins, J., 15, 83, 91, 130
Johnson, W., 140
John-Steiner, V., 124
Jones, G., 76
*Just Imagine,* 190

## K

Kaminsky, S., 114
Kamm, K., 72
Kappos, Paulette Condos, 186
Karlin, R., 63
Karlsen, B., 178
Kaufman, J., 66
Kenworthy Educational Services, Inc.,
  190
King, Carol L., 112, 192
King, M., 67, 68, 118, 156
Kintsch, W., 29
Kirk, E., 17
Knowledge
  base of, 7, 42
  cognitive, 22
  experiential, 22
  linguistic, 22
  metareading base of, 7
  pragmatic, 71
  semantic, 71
  world, 23, 28, 31, 83